BLOODAXE POETRY INTRODUCTIONS: 3

Books by Neil Astley

ANTHOLOGIES

Staying Alive: real poems for unreal times
(Bloodaxe Books, 2002; Miramax Books, USA, 2003)

Pleased to See Me: 69 very sexy poems (Bloodaxe Books, 2002)

Do Not Go Gentle: poems for funerals (Bloodaxe Books, 2003)

Being Alive: the sequel to Staying Alive (Bloodaxe Books, 2004)

Passionfood: 100 Love Poems (Bloodaxe Books, 2005)

Soul Food: nourishing poems for starved minds,
with Pamela Robertson-Pearce (Bloodaxe Books, 2007)

Earth Shattering: ecopoems (Bloodaxe Books, 2007)

BLOODAXE POETRY INTRODUCTIONS

1: *Elizabeth Alexander, Moniza Alvi, Imtiaz Dharker, Jackie Kay* (2006)

2: *Hans Magnus Enzensberger, Miroslav Holub, Marin Sorescu, Tomas Tranströmer* (2006)

3: *Jack Gilbert, Jane Hirshfield, Galway Kinnell, W.S. Merwin* (2007)

FURTHER TITLES TO BE ANNOUNCED

NOVELS

The End of My Tether (Flambard Press, 2002; Scribner, 2003)

The Sheep Who Changed the World (Flambard Press, 2005)

BLOODAXE POETRY INTRODUCTIONS

3

edited by
NEIL ASTLEY

BLOODAXE BOOKS

ISBN: 978 1 85224 767 6

First published 2007 by
Bloodaxe Books Ltd,
Highgreen,
Tarset,
Northumberland NE48 1RP.

www.bloodaxebooks.com
For further information about Bloodaxe titles please visit our website or write to the above address for a catalogue.

Bloodaxe Books Ltd acknowledges the financial assistance of Arts Council England, North East.

SPECIAL THANKS
To Alison Davis, especially, for thinking up this series, and to Kennet Havgaard for his portraits used on the covers (of people unconnected with the books or authors featured).

Cover printing by J. Thomson Colour Printers Ltd, Glasgow.

Printed in Great Britain by
Bell & Bain Limited, Glasgow, Scotland.

CONTENTS

JACK GILBERT

7 *Introduction*
13 Not Part of Literature
13 All the Way from There to Here
14 Leaving Monolithos
14 Hunger
15 Measuring the Tyger
16 Tear It Down
16 The Great Fires
17 Searching for Pittsburgh
18 The Spirit and the Soul
19 Alone
19 Gift Horses
20 Michiko Dead
21 I Imagine the Gods
22 A Brief for the Defense
22 Halloween
23 Elegy for Bob
24 Failing and Flying
25 Transgressions
26 'Tis Here! 'Tis Here! 'Tis Gone
27 The Lost Hotels of Paris
27 Music Is Only in the Piano When It Is Being Played
28 Refusing Heaven

JANE HIRSHFIELD

29 *Introduction*
35 For What Binds Us
35 The Weighing
36 *Da Capo*
37 Three Foxes by the Edge of the Field at Twilight
37 Manners/Rwanda
39 Each Moment a White Bull Steps Shining into the World
40 The Poet
41 Three Times My Life Has Opened
41 The Envoy
42 Habit
43 In Praise of Coldness
44 Pillow
45 For Horses, Horseflies
45 Optimism
46 Tree
46 Flowering Vetch
47 Theology
48 Vilnius
48 Burlap Sack

49 In a Room with Five People, Six Griefs
49 The Bell Zygmunt
50 It Was Like This: You Were Happy

GALWAY KINNELL
51 *Introduction*
57 The Bear
59 After Making Love We Hear Footsteps
60 Saint Francis and the Sow
61 Daybreak
61 Blackberry Eating
62 The Road Between Here and There
63 Prayer
63 That Silent Evening
64 Oatmeal
65 Last Gods
66 *from* When One Has Lived Alone a Long Time
68 Parkinson's Disease
69 Rapture
70 Everyone Was in Love
71 How Could She Not
72 Insomniac
73 Why Regret

W.S. MERWIN
75 *Introduction*
81 Learning a Dead Language
82 Grandmother Watching at Her Window
82 My Friends
84 The River of Bees
85 For the Anniversary of My Death
85 For a Coming Extinction
86 A Contemporary
87 Birdie
88 Yesterday
89 Unknown Forebear
90 Late Spring
91 Place
92 Losing a Language
93 Waves in August
93 In Time
94 To the Soul
95 To the Dust of the Road
95 To the Words
96 By Dark

JACK GILBERT

JULIO GRANDA

Jack Gilbert has always been a total outsider in American poetry, defiantly unfashionable and publishing only four books in five decades. Initially associated with the Beats, he left America after winning the Yale Younger Poets prize with *Views of Jeopardy*, eking out a living for some years on Greek islands. His second collection, *Monolithos*, appeared twenty years later in 1982, but he made his strongest impression on American readers with the late work published in his last two books, *The Great Fires: Poems 1982-1992* (1994) and *Refusing Heaven* (2005).

Jack Gilbert writes compellingly about passion, loss and loneliness. His poems are filled with a sense of wonder at existence and with his surprise at finding happiness – despite grief, struggle and alienation – in a life spent in luminous understanding of his own blessings and shortcomings. His work is both a rebellious assertion of clarity and a profound affirmation of the world in all its aspects. His poems are about being alive: the nature of the self, the life he lives and the people he loves. According to Dan Albergotti, 'Gilbert's inward journey has always been less about himself and more about understanding the universal human heart unpolluted by the distractions and temptations of modern life. He has given up convenience and ease to record the depth of a human life for the good of us all' (*Borderlands*, 25, Fall/Winter 2005).

Born in Pittsburgh, Pennsylvania, in 1925, he grew up during the Depression. His father died when Jack was 10, after falling out of the window of a Prohibition-era drinking club. Raised by his mother with three siblings, he began working with his uncle, fumigating houses with cyanide. After dropping out of high school, he continued working as an exterminator, sold brushes door to door and worked in a steel mill. At 15 he discovered Eliot and Pound, and started writing poetry. 'I was kind of a strange boy to be in Pittsburgh,' he told the *Paris Review*: 'I spent so much time reading. [...] I had such curiosity. And you might not think it, but the power of Pittsburgh, the grandeur, those two great rivers, was magnificent. Even working in the steel mills. Giant converters hundreds of feet hight. Every night, the sky looked enormous. It was a torrent of flames – of fire. The place that Pittsburgh used to be had such scale. [...] Everything was grand, heroic. Everything seemed to be gigantic in Pittsburgh – the people, the history. Sinuousness. Power. Substance. Meaningfulness.'

Gilbert failed freshman English eight times, but was accepted by the University of Pittsburgh thanks to a clerical error, and encouraged in his writing by fellow student Gerald Stern, but dropped out in 1946 to decamp to Paris, where he lived rough for a time. He eventually returned to the States, finishing college at Pittsburgh, and then did some teaching and worked with photographer Ansel Adams before moving to Italy, where he met his first great love, artist Gianna Gelmetti.

In 1954 he left Italy for San Francisco, where he lived for seven years 'like a hippie without drugs', taking part in Jack Spicer's famous 'Poetry as Magic' workshops and attending Kenneth Rexroth's Tuesday salon. Gilbert was by now extremely well read, and had very definite ideas about poetry. He and Allen Ginsberg argued so often that Ginsberg once took a bus across the bay to Sausalito, walking up rough tracks and through woods to reach the abandoned house where Gilbert was then living, to demand that he read a new poem. 'Finally, this is really beautiful, wonderful stuff,' Gilbert told him. It was the first two pages of 'Howl', soon to become the title-poem of Ginsberg's first book, published by City Lights in 1956.

Gilbert himself was always more interested in writing than publishing, viewing the whole poetry circus with some distaste, as he later commented: 'Most poets in America today are concerned with their career as poets far more than with their poetry.' By the time *Views of Jeopardy* was published in 1962, he was living in New York. With his first book nominated for a Pulitzer – and lauded by Dudley Fitts, Stanley Kunitz, Denise Levertov, Theodore Roethke, Muriel

Rukeyser and Stephen Spender – Gilbert was suddenly the most gifted new voice in American poetry, and was even photographed for *Glamour* and *Vogue*. He hated all the attention, and a Guggenheim Fellowship gave him the means of escape, knowing he could make the $5000 award go a long way.

In 1966 he left for Greece with Linda Gregg, a young poet from his San Francisco writing class, and they lived on Paros and Santorini, as well as briefly in Denmark and England, until separating in 1971. Back in San Francisco, Gilbert met and married his third great love and influence, sculptor Michiko Nogami; they moved to Japan, where he taught at Rikkyo University until 1975, when he took up a lecturing post (in American literature) for the US State Department, and they set off on a tour of 15 countries. In 1982, after eleven years of marriage, Michiko Nogami died of cancer at 36. Each of Gilbert's books has a presiding muse: Gelmetti celebrated in *Views of Jeopardy* and *Monolithos*; Gregg also in *Monolithos* (Greek for 'single stone', referring to the landscape on Santorini); Nogami elegised in *The Great Fires*; and all three present in *Refusing Heaven*. Gregg remains a key influence: 'She was the most valuable person in my life. She's the most important person in the world to me.'

Although Gilbert has never actively promoted his poetry, and only published sporadically, he has written almost continuously for over 50 years, with much of his success due to help from friends and other champions. He only won the Yale Younger Poets prize – at the age of 37 – because Gelmetti's brother-in-law Cleveland Moffett gave him the form and stamped addressed envelope to send in with his sheaf of poems. Gordon Lish then devoted 28 pages to a feature on Gilbert in the first issue of his journal *Genesis West*. Twenty years later, *Monolithos* came about because he'd sent some poems as a Christmas present to Lish, who got them published in *Esquire*, and then dragged the rest of the book out of him. *Monolithos* won the Stanley Kunitz Prize and the *American Poetry Review* Prize. All four of Gilbert's collections were nominated for a Pulitzer Prize. *The Great Fires*, which personal grief made possible, earned him a Lannan Literary Award. Eleven years later, *Refusing Heaven* – which Linda Gregg had asked him for – won the National Book Critics Circle Award and the *Los Angeles Times* Book Prize. Alice Quinn at *The New Yorker* had published nine of the poems ahead of publication, and her advocacy – along with that of Linda Gregg and David Semanki – led to Gilbert's first UK publication, *Transgressions: Selected Poems* (Bloodaxe Books, 2006), which draws on all his books. Now 82, Gilbert has a place to live – in Northampton, Massachusetts – thanks to another friend, Henry Lyman.

THREE COMMENTS BY JACK GILBERT

from The Landscape of American Poetry in 1965

Poetry, for me, is a witnessing to magnitude. It is the art of making urgent values manifest, and of imposing them on the reader. It is the housing of these values in poems so they will exist with maximum pressure, and for the longest time. It is the craft of doing so in structures that are a delight in themselves. And it is the mystery of fashioning poems in such a way that the form and the content are one.

What poetry chiefly is *not* for me is an entertainment. I recognise that there are other ways than mine to approach poetry: that for many it is an esthetic recreation, the making of beautiful objects; or it is the congenial play of imagination over a subject; or it is an exercise in expertise. It is not so for me. There is a voice in me that stubbornly sings of a largeness beyond formal considerations. Sings of love and death, god and evil, lust, honor, and all the other major business of life. [...] I am convinced poetry does make things happen – finally. I believe poetry deals with life. With my life. That it gives me my life more fully, and that it helps me in the direction in which I must proceed. Poetry is not, for me, a beautiful alternative to living.

This position is not fashionable in America today. The prevailing mood, set by the critics and a consensus of the respectable poets, is one of modesty. Most poets aspire to the adequate poem, not the important one. A masterpiece is thought of as something people used to write. And the critics, being nearly all scholarly sedentary men, have imposed an esthetic which insists that the primary values in poetry are those most available to a sedentary, scholarly life. For these critics, a poem is (as Robert Creeley says) 'a machine of manner': a formal construct in which the content is ancillary. [...]

The Beat poets, the Black Mountain people, and the New York group are generally self-indulgent. All but the very best are content with the approximate poem. They produce a flood of trivial poems that don't even have the excuse of technical finish. If the academic poets often seem to be doing something very well that isn't worth doing at all, these others tend to deal with matters of real importance with slovenliness. [...]

I do not speak so exigently of the present poetry in America from an easy impulse to find fault. Rather I do so out of love for and loyalty to the quality of the poetry which was produced in the United States in the first half of this century; and in the belief that such an insistence on excellence is the best way to produce equally great poetry in the next fifty years. Finally, I so insist out of admiration for those poets who are already at work on such poetry; poets like Robert Lowell, Robert Creeley, Stanley Kunitz, Robert Duncan, Allen Ginsberg, and Richard Wilbur. Praise to them.

from Real Nouns (1984)

The plain style that was so common until recently in this country is a reflection of the North American sensibility as well as a legacy from Whitman. Which in turn have roots farther back in the Protestant, North-European, Anglo-Saxon soul. A kind of ancestral mistrust of easy eloquence, bright colors and slack beauty.

Besides which, you must remember I grew up in Pittsburgh, Pennsylvania: a city of rusted iron, brutal winters, old trains at night, robber barons and steel mills. Not a place for charm or decoration (But a major place. Three impressive rivers, grand romantic summer storms, dinosaurs and unmistakable reality.)

I don't mean it was grim or that I came out damaged. I came out of Pittsburgh the only serious romantic I've ever met, a person who woke up happy nearly every day for 35 years after leaving – even though always conscious of mortality.

But whether these are the cause or not, poetry has always been a serious matter for me. I don't get off on it. [...] I'm trying to explain why my poetry seems 'stripped' to you. Poetry for me does not come from an instinct to play, as Auden insisted it did and as all the psychologists I know of who have studied creativity assume it does. Poetry, for me, is about something important; and I am in love with trying to implement that importance.

from Interview with *Paris Review* (2005)

I think serious poems should make something happen that's not correct or entertaining or clever. I want something that matters to my heart, and I don't mean 'Linda left me'. I don't want that. I'll write that poem, but that's not what I'm talking about. I'm talking about being in danger – as we all are – of dying. How can you spend your life on games or intricately accomplished things? And politics? Politics is fine. There's a place to care for the injustice of the world, but that's not what the poem is about. The poem is about the heart. Not the heart as in 'I'm in love' or 'my girl cheated on me' – I mean the conscious heart, the fact that we are the only things in the entire universe that know true consciousness. [...]

The most important day in my career as a writer was when Linda said, Did you ever think of listening to your poems? And my poetry changed. I didn't give up making precreated poetry, but you have to write a poem the way you ride a horse – you have to know what to do with it. You have to be in charge of a horse or it will eat all day – you'll never get it back to the barn. But if you tell the horse how to be a horse, if you force it, the horse will probably break a leg. The horse and rider have to be together. [...]

Oh, I like ornament at the right time, but I don't want a poem to be made out of decoration. If you like that kind of poetry, more power to you, but it doesn't interest me. When I read the poems that matter to me, it stuns me how much the presence of the heart – in all its forms – is endlessly available there. To experience ourselves in an important way just knocks me out. It puzzles me why people have given that up for cleverness. Some of them are ingenious, more ingenious than I am, but so many of them aren't any good at being alive. [...]

A lot of poets don't have any poems to write. After their first book, what are they going to do? They can't keep saying their hearts are broken. They start to write poems about childhood. Then what do they do? Some of it is just academic poetry – they learn how to write the poem perfectly. But I don't think anybody should be criticised because their taste is different from mine. Such poems are extraordinarily deft. There's a lot of art in them. But I don't understand where the meat is. I don't know what I'm supposed to do with this kind of poetry. It won't change my life, so why should I read it? Why should I write it? [...]

The hard part for me is to find the poem – a poem that matters. To find what the poem knows that's special. I may think of writing about the same thing that everyone does, but I really like to write a poem that hasn't been written. And I don't mean its shape. I want to experience or discover ways of feeling that are fresh. I love it when I have perceived something fresh about being human and being happy.

Ezra Pound said 'make it new'. The great tragedy of that saying is he left out the essential word. It should be make it *importantly* new. So much of the time people are just aiming for novelty, surprise. I like to think that I've understood, that I've learned about something that matters – what the world should be, what life should be.

SOURCES: 'Jack Gilbert and the Landscape of American Poetry in 1965', *Contemporary American Poetry*, Voice of America Forum Lectures (1965). 'Real Nouns' (addressed to Father Alberto Huerta), *19 New American Poets of the Golden Gate*, ed. Philip Dow (Harcourt Brace Jovanovich, 1984). Interview with Sarah Fay, 'The Art of Poetry No.91', *The Paris Review*, 47 no.175 (Fall/Winter 2005).

Not Part of Literature

Monolithos was four fisherman huts along the water,
a miniature villa closed for years, and our farmhouse
a hundred feet behind. Hot fields of barley, grapes,
and tomatoes stretching away three flat miles
to where the rest of the island used to be.
Where the few people live above the great cliffs.
A low mountain to the south and beyond that the earth
filled with pictures of Atlantis. On our wrong side
of the island were no people, cars, plumbing, or lights.
The summer skies and Mediterranean constantly. No trees.
Me cleaning squid. Linda getting up from a chair.

All the Way from There to Here

From my hill I look down on the freeway and over
to a gull lifting black against the grey ridge.
It lifts slowly higher and enters the bright sky.
Surely our long, steady dying brings us to a state
of grace. What else can I call this bafflement?

From here I deal with my irrelevance to love.
With the bewildering tenderness of which I am
composed. The sun goes down and comes up again.
The moon comes up and goes down. I live
with the morning air and the different airs of night.
I begin to grow old.

The ships put out and are lost.
Put out and are lost.
Leaving me with their haunting awkwardness
and the imperfection of birds. While all the time
I work to understand this happiness I have come into.

What I remember of my nine-story fall
down through the great fir is the rush of green.
And the softness of my regret in the ambulance going
to my nearby death, looking out at the trees leaving me.

What I remember of my crushed spine
is seeing Linda faint again and again,
sliding down the white X-ray room wall
as my sweet body flailed on the steel table
unable to manage the bulk of pain. That
and waiting in the years after for the burning
in my fingertips, which would announce,
the doctors said, the beginning of paralysis.

What I remember best of the four years of watching
in Greece and Denmark and London and Greece is Linda
making lunch. Her blondeness and ivory coming up
out of the blue Aegean. Linda walking with me daily
across the island from Monolithos to Thíra and back.
That's what I remember most of death:
the gentleness of us in that bare Greek Eden,
the beauty as the marriage steadily failed.

Leaving Monolithos

They were cutting the spring barley by fistfuls
when we came. Boys drove horses and mules over it
all day in threshing pits under the powerful sky.
They came from their white village on the horizon
for tomatoes in June. And later for grapes.
Now they are plowing in the cold wind. Yesterday
I burned my papers by the wall. This morning I look
back at the lone, shuttered farmhouse. Sun rising
over the volcano. At the full moon above the sea.

Hunger

Digging into the apple
with my thumbs.
Scraping out the clogged nails
and digging deeper.

Refusing the moon color.
Refusing the smell and memories.
Digging in with the sweet juice
running along my hands unpleasantly.
Refusing the sweetness.
Turning my hands to gouge out chunks.
Feeling the juice sticky
on my wrists. The skin itching.
Getting to the wooden part.
Getting to the seeds.
Going on.
Not taking anyone's word for it.
Getting beyond the seeds.

Measuring the Tyger

Barrels of chains. Sides of beef stacked in vans.
Water buffalo dragging logs of teak in the river mud
outside Mandalay. Pantocrater in the Byzantium dome.
The mammoth overhead crane bringing slabs of steel
through the dingy light and roar to the giant shear
that cuts the adamantine three-quarter-inch plates
and they flop down. The weight of the mind fractures
the girders and piers of the spirit, spilling out
the heart's melt. Incandescent ingots big as cars
trundling out of titanic mills, red slag scaling off
the brighter metal in the dark. The Monongahela River
below, night's sheen on its belly. Silence except
for the machinery clanging deeper in us. You will
love again, people say. Give it time. Me with time
running out. Day after day of the everyday.
What they call real life, made of eighth-inch gauge.
Newness strutting around as if it were significant.
Irony, neatness and rhyme pretending to be poetry.
I want to go back to that time after Michiko's death
when I cried every day among the trees. To the real.
To the magnitude of pain, of being that much alive.

Tear It Down

We find out the heart only by dismantling what
the heart knows. By redefining the morning,
we find a morning that comes just after darkness.
We can break through marriage into marriage.
By insisting on love we spoil it, get beyond
affection and wade mouth-deep into love.
We must unlearn the constellations to see the stars.
But going back toward childhood will not help.
The village is not better than Pittsburgh.
Only Pittsburgh is more than Pittsburgh.
Rome is better than Rome in the same way the sound
of raccoon tongues licking the inside walls
of the garbage tub is more than the stir
of them in the muck of the garbage. Love is not
enough. We die and are put into the earth forever.
We should insist while there is still time. We must
eat through the wildness of her sweet body already
in our bed to reach the body within that body.

The Great Fires

Love is apart from all things.
Desire and excitement are nothing beside it.
It is not the body that finds love.
What leads us there is the body.
What is not love provokes it.
What is not love quenches it.
Love lays hold of everything we know.
The passions which are called love
also change everything to a newness
at first. Passion is clearly the path
but does not bring us to love.
It opens the castle of our spirit
so that we might find the love which is
a mystery hidden there.
Love is one of many great fires.

Passion is a fire made of many woods,
each of which gives off its special odor
so we can know the many kinds
that are not love. Passion is the paper
and twigs that kindle the flames
but cannot sustain them. Desire perishes
because it tries to be love.
Love is eaten away by appetite.
Love does not last, but it is different
from the passions that do not last.
Love lasts by not lasting.
Isaiah said each man walks in his own fire
for his sins. Love allows us to walk
in the sweet music of our particular heart.

Searching for Pittsburgh

The fox pushes softly, blindly through me at night,
between the liver and the stomach. Comes to the heart
and hesitates. Considers and then goes around it.
Trying to escape the mildness of our violent world.
Goes deeper, searching for what remains of Pittsburgh
in me. The rusting mills sprawled gigantically
along three rivers. The authority of them.
The gritty alleys where we played every evening were
stained pink by the inferno always surging in the sky,
as though Christ and the Father were still fashioning
the Earth. Locomotives driving through the cold rain,
lordly and bestial in their strength. Massive water
flowing morning and night throughout a city
girded with ninety bridges. Sumptuous-shouldered,
sleek-thighed, obstinate and majestic, unquenchable.
All grip and flood, mighty sucking and deep-rooted grace.
A city of brick and tired wood. Ox and sovereign spirit.
Primitive Pittsburgh. Winter month after month telling
of death. The beauty forcing us as much as harshness.
Our spirits forged in that wilderness, our minds forged
by the heart. Making together a consequence of America.
The fox watched me build my Pittsburgh again and again.

In Paris afternoons on Buttes-Chaumont. On Greek islands with their fields of stone. In beds with women, sometimes, amid their gentleness. Now the fox will live in our ruined house. My tomatoes grow ripe among weeds and the sound of water. In this happy place my serious heart has made.

The Spirit and the Soul

It should have been the family that lasted.
Should have been my sister and my peasant mother.
But it was not. They were the affection,
not the journey. It could have been my father,
but he died too soon. Gelmetti and Gregg
and Nogami lasted. It was the newness of me,
and the newness after that, and newness again.
It was the important love and the serious lust.
It was Pittsburgh that lasted. The iron and fog
and sooty brick houses. Not Aunt Mince and Pearl,
but the black-and-white winters with their girth
and geological length of cold. Streets ripped
apart by ice and emerging like wounded beasts when
the snow finally left in April. Freight trains
with their steam locomotives working at night.
Summers the size of crusades. When I was a boy,
I saw downtown a large camera standing in front
of the William Pitt Hotel or pointed at Kaufmann's
Department Store. Usually around midnight,
but the people still going by. The camera set
slow enough that cars and people left no trace.
The crowds in Rome and Tokyo and Manhattan
did not last. But the empty streets of Perugia,
my two bowls of bean soup on Kos, and Pimpaporn
Charionpanith lasted. The plain nakedness of Anna
in Denmark remains in me forever. The wet lilacs
on Highland Avenue when I was fourteen. Carrying
Michiko dead in my arms. It is not about the spirit.
The spirit dances, comes and goes. But the soul
is nailed to us like lentils and fatty bacon lodged
under the ribs. What lasted is what the soul ate.

The way a child knows the world by putting it
part by part into his mouth. As I tried to gnaw
my way into the Lord, working to put my heart
against that heart. Lying in the wheat at night,
letting the rain after all the dry months have me.

Alone

I never thought Michiko would come back
after she died. But if she did, I knew
it would be as a lady in a long white dress.
It is strange that she has returned
as somebody's dalmatian. I meet
the man walking her on a leash
almost every week. He says good morning
and I stoop down to calm her. He said
once that she was never like that with
other people. Sometimes she is tethered
on their lawn when I go by. If nobody
is around, I sit on the grass. When she
finally quiets, she puts her head in my lap
and we watch each other's eyes as I whisper
in her soft ears. She cares nothing about
the mystery. She likes it best when
I touch her head and tell her small
things about my days and our friends.
That makes her happy the way it always did.

Gift Horses

He lives in the barrens, in dying neighborhoods
and negligible countries. None with an address.
But still the Devil finds him. Kills the wife
or spoils the marriage. Publishes each place
and makes it popular, makes it better, makes it

unusable. Brings news of friends, all defeated,
most sick or sad without reasons. Shows him
photographs of the beautiful women in old movies
whose luminous faces sixteen feet tall looked out
at the boy in the dark where he grew his heart.
Brings pictures of what they look like now.
Says how lively they are, and brave despite their age.
Taking away everything. For the Devil is commissioned
to harm, to keelhaul us with loss, with knowledge
of how all things splendid are disfigured by small
and small. Yet he allows us to eat roast goat
on the mountain above Parakia. Lets us stumble
for the first time, unprepared, onto the buildings
of Palladio in moonlight. Maybe because he is not
good at his job. I believe he loves us against
his will. Because of the women and how the men
struggle to hear inside them. Because we construe
something important from trees and locomotives,
smell weeds on a hot July afternoon and are augmented.

Michiko Dead

He manages like somebody carrying a box
that is too heavy, first with his arms
underneath. When their strength gives out,
he moves the hands forward, hooking them
on the corners, pulling the weight against
his chest. He moves his thumbs slightly
when the fingers begin to tire, and it makes
different muscles take over. Afterward,
he carries it on his shoulder, until the blood
drains out of the arm that is stretched up
to steady the box and the arm goes numb. But now
the man can hold underneath again, so that
he can go on without ever putting the box down.

I Imagine the Gods

I imagine the gods saying, We will
make it up to you. We will give you
three wishes, they say. Let me see
the squirrels again, I tell them.
Let me eat some of the great hog
stuffed and roasted on its giant spit
and put out, steaming, into the winter
of my neighborhood when I was usually
too broke to afford even the hundred grams
I ate so happily walking up the cobbles,
past the Street of the Moon
and the Street of the Birdcage-Makers,
the Street of Silence and the Street
of the Little Pissing. We can give you
wisdom, they say in their rich voices.
Let me go at last to Hugette, I say,
the Algerian student with her huge eyes
who timidly invited me to her room
when I was too young and bewildered
that first year in Paris.
Let me at least fail at my life.
Think, they say patiently, we could
make you famous again. Let me fall
in love one last time, I beg them.
Teach me mortality, frighten me
into the present. Help me to find
the heft of these days. That the nights
will be full enough and my heart feral.

A Brief for the Defense

Sorrow everywhere. Slaughter everywhere. If babies
are not starving someplace, they are starving
somewhere else. With flies in their nostrils.
But we enjoy our lives because that's what God wants.
Otherwise the mornings before summer dawn would not
be made so fine. The Bengal tiger would not
be fashioned so miraculously well. The poor women
at the fountain are laughing together between
the suffering they have known and the awfulness
in their future, smiling and laughing while somebody
in the village is very sick. There is laughter
every day in the terrible streets of Calcutta,
and the women laugh in the cages of Bombay.
If we deny our happiness, resist our satisfaction,
we lessen the importance of their deprivation.
We must risk delight. We can do without pleasure,
but not delight. Not enjoyment. We must have
the stubbornness to accept our gladness in the ruthless
furnace of this world. To make injustice the only
measure of our attention is to praise the Devil.
If the locomotive of the Lord runs us down,
we should give thanks that the end had magnitude.
We must admit there will be music despite everything.
We stand at the prow again of a small ship
anchored late at night in the tiny port
looking over to the sleeping island: the waterfront
is three shuttered cafés and one naked light burning.
To hear the faint sound of oars in the silence as a rowboat
comes slowly out and then goes back is truly worth
all the years of sorrow that are to come.

Halloween

There were a hundred wild people in Allen's
three-story house. He was sitting at a small
table in the kitchen quietly eating something.

Alone, except for Orlovsky's little brother
who was asleep with his face against the wall.
Allen wearing a red skullcap, and a loose bathrobe
over his nakedness. Shoulder-length hair
and a chest-length, oily beard.
No one was within fifteen years of him. Destroyed
like the rest of that clan. His remarkable
talent destroyed. The fine mind grown more
and more simple. Buddhist chants, impoverishing
poems. There are no middle tones in the paintings
of children. Chekhov said he didn't want
the audience to cry, but to see. Allen showing
me his old man's bald scalp. A kind of love.
Aachen is a good copy of a mediocre building.
Architects tried for two thousand years to find
a way to put a dome on a square base.

Elegy for Bob

(Jean McLean)

Only you and I still stand in the snow on Highland Avenue
in Pittsburgh waiting for the blundering iron streetcars
that never came. Only you know how the immense storms
over the Allegheny and Monongahela rivers were the scale
I wanted. Nobody but you remembers Peabody High School.
You shared my youth in Paris and the hills above Como.
And later, in Seattle. It was you playing the aria from
Don Giovanni over and over, filling the forest of Puget
Sound with the music. You in the front room and me
upstairs with your discarded wife in my bed. The sound
of your loneliness pouring over our happy bodies.
You were with your third wife when I was in Perugia
six months later, but were in love with somebody else.
We searched for her in Munich, the snow falling again.
You trying to decide when to kill yourself. All of it
finally bringing us to San Francisco. To the vast
decaying white house. No sound of Mozart coming up
from there. No alleluias in you anymore. No longer
will you waltz under the chandeliers in Paris salons

drunk with champagne and the Greek girl as the others stand along the mirrored walls. The men watching with fury, the eyes of the women inscrutable. No one else speaks the language of those years. No one remembers you as the Baron. The streetcars have finished the last run, and I am walking home. Thinking love is not refuted because it comes to an end.

Failing and Flying

Everyone forgets that Icarus also flew.
It's the same when love comes to an end,
or the marriage fails and people say
they knew it was a mistake, that everybody
said it would never work. That she was
old enough to know better. But anything
worth doing is worth doing badly.
Like being there by that summer ocean
on the other side of the island while
love was fading out of her, the stars
burning so extravagantly those nights that
anyone could tell you they would never last.
Every morning she was asleep in my bed
like a visitation, the gentleness in her
like antelope standing in the dawn mist.
Each afternoon I watched her coming back
through the hot stony field after swimming,
the sea light behind her and the huge sky
on the other side of that. Listened to her
while we ate lunch. How can they say
the marriage failed? Like the people who
came back from Provence (when it was Provence)
and said it was pretty but the food was greasy.
I believe Icarus was not failing as he fell,
but just coming to the end of his triumph.

Transgressions

He thinks about how important the sinning was,
how much his equity was in simply being alive.
Like the sloth. The days and nights wasted,
doing nothing important adding up to
the favorite years. Long hot afternoons
watching ants while the cicadas railed
in the Chinese elm about the brevity of life.
Indolence so often when no one was watching.
Wasting June mornings with the earth singing
all around. Autumn afternoons doing nothing
but listening to the siren voices of streams
and clouds coaxing him into the sweet happiness
of leaving all of it alone. Using up what
little time we have, relishing our mortality,
waltzing slowly without purpose. Neglecting
the future. Content to let the garden fail
and the house continue on in its usual disorder.
Yes, and coveting his neighbors' wives.
Their clean hair and soft voices. The seraphim
he was sure were in one of the upstairs rooms.
Hesitant occasions of pride, feeling himself feeling.
Waking in the night and lying there. Discovering
the past in the wonderful stillness. The other,
older pride. Watching the ambulance take away
the man whose throat he had crushed. Above all,
his greed. Greed of time, of being. This world,
the pine woods stretching all brown or bare
on either side of the railroad tracks in the winter
twilight. Him feeling the cold, sinfully unshriven.

’Tis Here! ’Tis Here! ’Tis Gone!

(The Nature of Presence)

A white horse, Linda Gregg wrote, is not a horse,
quoting what Hui Shih said twenty-three hundred
years ago. The thing is not its name, is not
the words. The painting of a pipe is not a pipe
regardless of what the title claims. An intelligent
poet in Iowa is frightened because she thinks
we are made of electrons. The Gianna Gelmetti
I loved was a presence ignited in a swarm
of energy, but the ghost living in the mansion
is not the building. Consciousness is not
matter dreaming. If all the stars were added
together they would still not know it’s spring.
The silence of the mountain is not our silence.
The sound of the earth will never be *Un Bel Di*.
We are a contingent occurrence. The white horse
in moonlight is more white than when it stands
in sunlight. And even then it depends on whether
a bell is ringing. The intimate body of the Valerie
I know is not the secret body my friend knows.
The luster of her breasts is conditional:
clothed or not, desired or too familiar.
The fact of them is mediated by morning
or the depth of night when it’s pouring down rain.
The reason we cannot enter the same woman
twice is not because the mesh of energy flexes.
It is a mystery separate from both matter
and electrons. It is not why the Linda
looking out over the Aegean is not the Linda
eating melon in Kentucky, nor explains how
the mind lives amid the rain without being
part of it. The dead lady Nogami-san lives now
only in me, in the momentary occasion I am.
Her whiteness in me is the color of pale amber
in winter light.

The Lost Hotels of Paris

The Lord gives everything and charges
by taking it back. What a bargain.
Like being young for a while. We are
allowed to visit hearts of women,
to go into their bodies so we feel
no longer alone. We are permitted
romantic love with its bounty and half-life
of two years. It is right to mourn
for the small hotels of Paris that used to be
when we used to be. My mansard looking
down on Notre Dame every morning is gone,
and me listening to the bell at night.
Venice is no more. The best Greek islands
have drowned in acceleration. But it's the having
not the keeping that is the treasure.
Ginsberg came to my house one afternoon
and said he was giving up poetry
because it told lies, that language distorts.
I agreed, but asked what we have
that gets it right even that much.
We look up at the stars and they are
not there. We see the memory
of when they were, once upon a time.
And that too is more than enough.

Music Is in the Piano Only When It Is Played

We are not one with this world. We are not
the complexity our body is, nor the summer air
idling in the big maple without purpose.
We are a shape the wind makes in these leaves
as it passes through. We are not the wood
any more than the fire, but the heat which is a marriage
between the two. We are certainly not the lake
nor the fish in it, but the something that is
pleased by them. We are the stillness when

a mighty Mediterranean noon subtracts even the voices
of insects by the broken farmhouse. We are evident
when the orchestra plays, and yet are not part
of the strings or brass. Like the song that exists
only in the singing, and is not the singer.
God does not live among the church bells,
but is briefly resident there. We are occasional
like that. A lifetime of easy happiness mixed
with pain and loss, trying always to name and hold
on to the enterprise underway in our chest.
Reality is not what we marry as a feeling. It is what
walks up the dirt path, through the excessive heat
and giant sky, the sea stretching away.
He continues past the nunnery to the old villa
where he will sit on the terrace with her, their sides
touching. In the quiet that is the music of that place,
which is the difference between silence and windlessness.

Refusing Heaven

The old women in black at early Mass in winter
are a problem for him. He could tell by their eyes
they have seen Christ. They make the kernel
of his being and the clarity around it
seem meager, as though he needs girders
to hold up his unusable soul. But he chooses
against the Lord. He will not abandon his life.
Not his childhood, not the ninety-two bridges
across the two rivers of his youth. Nor the mills
along the banks where he became a young man
as he worked. The mills are eaten away, and eaten
again by the sun and its rusting. He needs them
even though they are gone, to measure against.
The silver is worn down to the brass underneath
and is the better for it. He will gauge
by the smell of cement sidewalks after night rain.
He is like an old ferry dragged on to the shore,
a home in its smashed grandeur, with the giant beams
and joists. Like a wooden ocean out of control.
A beached heart. A cauldron of cooling melt.

JANE HIRSHFIELD

MARK MOFFETT

Jane Hirshfield is a visionary American writer whose poems ask nothing less than what it is to be human. Both sensual meditations and passionate investigations, they reveal complex truths in language luminous and precise. Rooted in the living world, her poems celebrate and elucidate a hard-won affirmation of our human fate. Born of a rigorous questioning of heart, spirit and mind, they have become indispensible to many American readers in navigating their own lives. Hers is a poetry of clarity and hybrid vigour, drawing deeply on English and American traditions but also those of world poetry. The poetries of modern and classical Greece, of Horace and Catullus, of classical China and Japan and Eastern Europe all resonate in Hirshfield's structures of thought and in her sensibilities.

Jane Hirshfield was born in 1953 in New York and has lived in northern California for the past 30 years. Her first book of poetry published in the UK was *Each Happiness Ringed by Lions: Selected Poems* (Bloodaxe Books, 2005), which draws on five collections: *Alaya* (1982), *Of Gravity & Angels* (1988), *The October Palace* (1994), *The Lives of the Heart* (1997) and *Given Sugar, Given Salt* (2001). Her latest collection, *After* (Bloodaxe Books, 2006), a Poetry Book Society

Choice, was shortlisted for the T.S. Eliot Prize. She has won numerous literary awards.

Her collection of essays, *Nine Gates: Entering the Mind of Poetry* was published by HarperCollins in 1997; her 2007 Newcastle/Bloodaxe Poetry Lectures, *Uncertainty, Hiddenness, Surprise: Three Generative Energies of Poetry*, will be published in 2008. She has edited and co-translated several books collecting the work of women poets of the past: *The Ink Dark Moon: Love Poems by Ono no Komachi and Izumi Shikibu, Women of the Ancient Court of Japan* (1990); *Women in Praise of the Sacred: 43 Centuries of Spiritual Poetry by Women* (1994); and *Mirabai: Ecstatic Poems* (2004).

from Profile: Jane Hirshfield (1998)
by PETER HARRIS

Jane Hirshfield's career might be said to have begun in first grade, when she wrote on a large sheet of lined paper: 'I want to be a writer when I grow up.' She had forgotten all about this youthful resolve until she published her first book of poems, whereupon her mother startled her by pulling it out of a drawer. Uncertainty aside, not many writers have had, by age six, such a clear inkling of their calling. And looking back, it seems quite right that the first book she bought, at age nine, was a collection of haiku. That attraction to things Japanese surfaced again, at Princeton, where as an undergraduate she created an independent major: Creative Writing and Literature in Translation.

If one's destiny is shaped by fateful detours, the next period in Hirshfield's life seems a particularly fateful swerve. Shortly after graduating from college, she won the poetry contest of *The Nation* for work written while still an undergraduate. But instead of getting an MFA, she decided that the best, perhaps the only way for her to move forward was to study Zen. A few months were enough to teach her how little she knew, and after a year, she made the decision to enter monastic practice, during which time she knew she'd stop writing poetry altogether. 'I had to be willing to walk away from poetry, perhaps forever, before I felt like I could do it at all.' What began as a month's commitment turned into eight years study with the San Francisco Zen Center, including three years at Tassajara, living in deep wilderness without electricity, quite a change for someone born in Manhattan in 1953 and raised on the Lower East Side. [...]

The range of things to which she turns her mindfulness reminds one of a short poem she co-translates in *Women in Praise of the Sacred*. It is by Chiyo-ni, an 18th-century Buddhist: 'From the mind/of a single, long vine,/one hundred opening lives.' One of the most refreshing elements of Hirshfield's long vine is that its blossoms are colored by an astonishing variety of sources. Like many of her contemporaries, she writes free verse in American diction, and she loves Whitman, Dickinson, Kinnell, Bishop, Snyder and Hass – not to mention those other "American" influences, Neruda, Rilke, Miłosz – but it is her acquaintance with profoundly exotic sensibilities – from India, China, and especially Japan – that lend her work a distinct depth and undeniable air.

Her recent book of essays on poetry, *Nine Gates: Entering the Mind of Poetry*, does for poetry what Pound intended to do at the turn of the century: through juxtaposition of the familiar and the unknown, it reinvigorates our thinking about the possibilities of the art. One difference is that Hirshfield's remarks are more fully considered. Twelve years in gestation, two years in the re-writing, *Nine Gates* is surely one of the most eloquent books ever written about poetry. And even if it weren't, the range of its apposite allusions would set it apart. [...]

As to Hirshfield's own poetry and its influences, anyone with more than a passing acquaintance with Zen Buddhism can feel, and savor, its organic incorporation into her work. Thematically, for instance, the emphases on compassion, on the pre-existent unity of subject and object, on nature, on the self-sufficient suchness of being, on the daunting challenge of accepting transitoriness – all are central to Buddhism. Of course, every American poet after Pound and Williams owes a debt to the image-centered poetics of Japanese and Chinese verse. Hirshfield herself resists, rightly, being labelled a "Buddhist poet". Unlike, say, Gary Snyder, she pursues no doctrinal path and makes only a few allusions to the literature of Zen. One of the attractions for her of Zen monasticism was that the stage of sequestered, intensive study is designed to come to an end. Just as Zen itself merges with the ordinary, its students re-enter the world. At a certain point in one's practice, Hirshfield says, 'there is no Zen, only life'. [...]

When asked about the respective roles of nature and politics in her poetry, Hirshfield characteristically sees the two realms as related. Or rather, she proffers, then erases, a distinction between the natural and what she has called the 'chronicled world': 'One of the marks of being human is that we reside amidst all of the stories that we have created to examine our existence more thoroughly –

scientific, political, historical, psychological, mythic. At the same time we exist in a continuum with non-human being.' One of the effects of Zen training has been to de-center her inherited Western world-view. 'I am actually not all that human-centered. I know that many, many people would disagree with this stance. Both the Judeo-Christian and the Marxist worlds would disagree.' But for her, the natural and political are, in an absolute sense, not distinct. 'If you exploit nature you will exploit people. If you find somehow at the most fundamental level of being that your relationship to other people, other things, other animals, is a relationship of kinship then you perhaps will behave ethically in the world.' Because she dwells with this radical vision of kinship, her poems are only infrequently political, but hearteningly compassionate.

from Ambered Phrases: An Interview with Jane Hirshfield (2001)

by SHEL EVANS

SE: How does *Given Sugar, Given Salt* differ from some of your other collections of poetry?

JH: As soon as I began to write again after finishing *The Lives of the Heart*, I noticed a kind of climate change, a shift of inner weather and outer landscape, in how the poems looked at the world and in what they looked at. One of these "different" poems was 'The Silence', another 'Sleep'. An earlier poem prefigures this shift, an atypical longer poem, 'The Four-Postered Beds of Mycenae', which ponders invention, and includes, among other things, a description of many different kinds of light switches. Not my usual terrain. Many poems in this new book start off from something that began to be learned in that one. They hold a more extended and meditative unfolding, as if they'd settled into a gait meant for going some distance. Their world is also more peopled, more seated in the objects and events of ordinary domestic life than in earlier books. There's more actual speech, held in quotation marks. They also seem to possess – alongside what I hope is a full fidelity to feeling – a greater detachment. It goes with the lengthening of stride, in a way I can't quite explain, except that rhythms, pace, altered music are also alterations of thought and sensibility. Novalis once said, 'We spend the first half of our lives looking inward, the second half outward.' I think that is the shift most apparent in this new book. There's more looking outward.

SE: While you were working on these poems, what were some of your major influences? Were any particular books, poems, or other writers especially important?

JH: At this point in my writing life, many of my influences are abiding ones, and I can feel in my work the accumulated gleanings of every poet I've read. Many of my mentors are the obvious ones, a few might be less commonly thought of – Horace, say, whom I first fell in love with at 16, when I could read him in Latin.

But I can also name two poets who may have influenced this particular book more strongly, as I was reading deeply in each of them during the time some of the poems were being written. One, Borges, I had of course read before; but during the writing of *Given Sugar, Given Salt* I reread first an older selection of his poems, and then, by happy coincidence, a new *Collected Poems* came out just at that time. I made my way through that book very slowly, a poem or two a day, savoring and taking in the old trickster-master with all his love of arcane learnedness and embedded passions.

The second poet was the early 20th-century Portuguese poet Pessoa. I hadn't paid much attention to his poetry before, but the then-new Richard Zenith translation caught my eye in a bookstore. Pessoa's influence can be seen quite directly in the poems in this book whose titles mirror their first lines; but also in a wider way, in a point of overlap between his work and that of Borges: their stance of heightened detachment and perspective. And then one of Pessoa's personae (he called them 'heteronyms') writes strongly in the style of Horace and the Roman Epicureans…I don't seem to surrender any of my loves, in literature or in life. I remain in awe of the power of certain statements in Pessoa – the surface almost tautologically simple, the undermeaning somehow opening into a vastness.

I know some consider it bad form to admit to being influenced by work in translation, but a great many of my most powerful poetic encounters, especially in adult life, have come from poets working in other languages. I took in the English and American poets voraciously in high school, and also the Romans in Latin classes, then hungered for the world – the Chinese and Japanese, the Greeks, the Nahuatl, the Nordic and the Eastern Europeans. Miłosz, Herbert, Cavafy, Brecht. In plant breeding, they speak of "hybrid vigor"; among pound dogs, of the intelligence and health of mongrels. I think the same is true for poetry – no lineage is "pure" in any case, and a young writer wants to steep herself in as many varieties of mind-encounter and tongue-encounter and heart-encounter as she can.

JANE HIRSHFIELD

Comment on *After* (2006)

For me, the meaningful measure of poetry is the individual poem, and it is poems I write, not books. Yet a book holds the coherencies of the life that made it, and *After*'s parts respond to a particularly strong magnet. The period of its writing was filled with vanishments – the deaths of September 11 and the continuing violence of its aftermath; the disappeared amid earthquake and tsunami; an onslaught of more intimate deaths, both of family and loved friends. This collection is haunted by time, its continuance and its erasures. During these years, it seemed I could not assay the meanings of even the preposition 'to' – a word essentially of optimistic linkage – without finding myself arriving at 'dust to dust'.

Poetry, though, is aimed toward life, its gleam-light phosphorescence even in darkness, its restorative music and breadth. My poems each emerge from some distinct question, event, or fracturing of the lived day or night, but they take root equally in geology, biology, friendships, eros, metaphysics; in the Cézanne-planes of mind and heart; in the mountain each morning outside bedroom window. I want from my own poems what I want from the poems of others – entrance into a more fully inhabited life, one knowable with greater subtlety, force, and saturation.

Two specific types of poem appear in this book: the assays and pebbles. Mirroring forms, each hunts out thought and feeling through the alloy of outwardly and inwardly attuned observation.

The pebbles' mode is brevity, recalcitrance, dryness. As with a joke, koan, or riddle, they are a kind of pointing-toward, not fully realized until the reader completes the factoring, finding an after-response not yet on the page.

The assays are more peregrine, and their lineage falls somewhere between the prose meditation and certain odes. The word is cognate to 'essay'; I use the term, though, as it is used in chemistry – you assay a substance to discover what it is made of, what parts in what strengths. Such knowledge is the first stage of transformation.

Extract from 'Profile: Jane Hirshfield by Peter Harris': from *Ploughshares*, 75 vol. 24/1 (Spring 1998). Extract from 'Ambered Phrases: An Interview with Jane Hirshfield' by Shel Evans: from *Arts & Letters*, 7 (Spring 2002). Jane Hirshfield comment from *PBS Bulletin*, 211 (Winter 2006).

For What Binds Us

There are names for what binds us:
strong forces, weak forces.
Look around, you can see them:
the skin that forms in a half-empty cup,
nails rusting into the places they join,
joints dovetailed on their own weight.
The way things stay so solidly
wherever they've been set down –
and gravity, scientists say, is weak.

And see how the flesh grows back
across a wound, with a great vehemence,
more strong
than the simple, untested surface before.
There's a name for it on horses,
when it comes back darker and raised: proud flesh,

as all flesh
is proud of its wounds, wears them
as honors given out after battle,
small triumphs pinned to the chest –

And when two people have loved each other
see how it is like a
scar between their bodies,
stronger, darker, and proud;
how the black cord makes of them a single fabric
that nothing can tear or mend.

The Weighing

The heart's reasons
seen clearly,
even the hardest
will carry
its whip-marks and sadness
and must be forgiven.

As the drought-starved
eland forgives
the drought-starved lion
who finally takes her,
enters willingly then
the life she cannot refuse,
and is lion, is fed,
and does not remember the other.

So few grains of happiness
measured against all the dark
and still the scales balance.

The world asks of us
only the strength we have and we give it.
Then it asks more, and we give it.

Da Capo

Take the used-up heart like a pebble
and throw it far out.

Soon there is nothing left.
Soon the last ripple exhausts itself
in the weeds.

Returning home, slice carrots, onions, celery.
Glaze them in oil before adding
the lentils, water, and herbs.

Then the roasted chestnuts, a little pepper, the salt.
Finish with goat cheese and parsley. Eat.
You may do this, I tell you, it is permitted.
Begin again the story of your life.

Three Foxes by the Edge of the Field at Twilight

One ran,
her nose to the ground,
a rusty shadow
neither hunting nor playing.

One stood; sat; lay down; stood again.

One never moved,
except to turn her head a little as we walked.

Finally we drew too close,
and they vanished.
The woods took them back as if they had never been.

I wish I had thought to put my face to the grass.

But we kept walking,
speaking as strangers do when becoming friends.

There is more and more I tell no one,
strangers nor loves.
This slips into the heart
without hurry, as if it had never been.

And yet, among the trees, something has changed.

Something looks back from the trees,
and knows me for who I am.

Manners/Rwanda

They took the woman
and tied to one arm a child
to the other arm a child
to one leg a child
to the other leg a child –
you also read this in the paper –
and threw them all in.

No marks of damage, not one
on the five bodies,
which means of course
that they drowned,
which means of course
that she knew.
The river made its way
from higher ground toward lower
and carried them with decorum,
the way a river does,
it carries what it is given,
and because in the night
a border was crossed,
what was given then was
taken out with a pole.
It may have been untied
before being added
to the tally sheet with others
and given next
to the quicklime and earth,
but probably not.
There it will likely stay,
where it was carried,
the last contact
with anything living
a hand's continuing rising,
almost a waving,
almost a plea,
letting go after rolling it in.
The two beats of the fall
almost gentle,
a door being carefully opened,
quietly closed.
And though you too
are sickened, as even the river
is sickened, undrinkable now
with the human heart,
you also carry
what you were given with decorum.
Perhaps reminded later
by something mentioned
only in passing –
a large family,

a cat's toy of string –
you stop smiling a moment soon.
Across the table
someone notices,
but does not speak.
You watch his question rise
and seem to waver like a hand
about to act,
a hand about to change its mind,
then drop politely away.

Each Moment a White Bull Steps Shining into the World

If the gods bring to you
a strange and frightening creature,
accept the gift
as if it were one you had chosen.

Say the accustomed prayers,
oil the hooves well,
caress the small ears with praise.

Have the new halter of woven silver
embedded with jewels.
Spare no expense, pay what is asked,
when a gift arrives from the sea.

Treat it as you yourself
would be treated,
brought speechless and naked
into the court of a king.

And when the request finally comes,
do not hesitate even an instant –

Stroke the white throat,
the heavy, trembling dewlaps
you've come to believe were yours,
and plunge in the knife.

Not once
did you enter the pasture
without pause,
without yourself trembling.
That you came to love it, that was the gift.

Let the envious gods take back what they can.

The Poet

She is working now, in a room
not unlike this one,
the one where I write, or you read.
Her table is covered with paper.
The light of the lamp would be
tempered by a shade, where the bulb's
single harshness might dissolve,
but it is not, she has taken it off.
Her poems? I will never know them,
though they are the ones I most need.
Even the alphabet she writes in
I cannot decipher. Her chair –
Let us imagine whether it is leather
or canvas, vinyl or wicker. Let her
have a chair, her shadeless lamp,
the table. Let one or two she loves
be in the next room. Let the door
be closed, the sleeping ones healthy.
Let her have time, and silence,
enough paper to make mistakes and go on.

Three Times My Life Has Opened

Three times my life has opened.
Once, into darkness and rain.
Once, into what the body carries at all times within it and starts
to remember each time it enters the act of love.
Once, to the fire that holds all.
These three were not different.
You will recognise what I am saying or you will not.
But outside my window all day a maple has stepped from her leaves
like a woman in love with winter, dropping the colored silks.
Neither are we different in what we know.
There is a door. It opens. Then it is closed. But a slip of light
stays, like a scrap of unreadable paper left on the floor,
or the one red leaf the snow releases in March.

The Envoy

One day in that room, a small rat.
Two days later, a snake.

Who, seeing me enter,
whipped the long stripe of his
body under the bed,
then curled like a docile house-pet.

I don't know how either came or left.
Later, the flashlight found nothing.

For a year I watched
as something – terror? happiness? grief? –
entered and then left my body.

Not knowing how it came in,
Not knowing how it went out.

It hung where words could not reach it.
It slept where light could not go.
Its scent was neither snake nor rat,
neither sensualist nor ascetic.

There are openings in our lives
of which we know nothing.

Through them
the belled herds travel at will,
long-legged and thirsty, covered with foreign dust.

Habit

The shoes put on each time
left first, then right.

The morning potion's teaspoon
of sweetness stirred always
for seven circlings – no fewer, no more –
into the cracked blue cup.

Touching the pocket for wallet,
for keys,
before closing the door.

How did we come
to believe these small rituals' promise,
that we are today the selves we yesterday knew,
tomorrow will be?

How intimate and unthinking,
the way the toothbrush is shaken dry after use,
the part we wash first in the bath.

Which habits we learned from others
and which are ours alone we may never know.
Unbearable to acknowledge
how much they are themselves our fated life.

Open the traveling suitcase –

There the beloved red sweater,
bright tangle of necklace, earrings of amber.
Each confirming: I chose these, I.

But habit is different: it chooses.
And we, its good horse,
opening our mouths at even the sight of the bit.

In Praise of Coldness

'If you wish to move your reader,'
Chekhov wrote, 'you must write more coldly.'

Herakleitos recommended, 'A dry soul is best.'

And so at the center of many great works
is found a preserving dispassion,
like the vanishing point of quattrocento perspective,
or the tiny packets of desiccant enclosed
in a box of new shoes or seeds.

But still the vanishing point
is not the painting,
the silica is not the blossoming plant.

Chekhov, dying, read the timetables of trains.
To what more earthly thing could he have been faithful? –
Scent of rocking distances,
smoke of blue trees out the window,
hampers of bread, pickled cabbage, boiled meat.

Scent of the knowable journey.

Neither a person entirely broken
nor one entirely whole can speak.

In sorrow, pretend to be fearless. In happiness, tremble.

Pillow

Some pillows are made of down, feathers,
and striped cotton ticking,
some of wool or dried herb flowers,
others of thought.

The thought of a good sandwich
in the lunch bag, for instance –
provolone slices and garden tomato,
a little Dijon and mayonnaise – can be a pillow,

comforting as the memory of being,
for one moment,
not entirely embarrassed to be human.

Able, say, to meet the gaze
of a cow or a horse with eyes neither arrogant
nor lowered, to offer a carrot
not as propitiation or bribe but simple friendship.

Friendship can be simple,
like the pillow of a horseshoe's lucky curve
above a door where it's needed.

'Here,' I said to my friend when he was dying.
'Here,' he replied.

There was nothing more to ask of one another,
though we spoke a while longer,
words like river pebbles, some black, some white,
wrapped in a handkerchief's tied-together purse.

I could not eat them,
so I put them under my pillow that night,
and slept well,
without dismay or turning,
though he would continue dying, though I would live.

His look, those days: plain as water, undeterred
by the ongoing disassemblage.
A little greedy, but also ready, prepared.

Whatever came, he told me, would be his own luck.

We held hands a time,
then together let go that touch,
together turned to our separate tasks,

like the two hands
of a person arranging the blankets and pillow
just so before sleeping,
settling the one day in order to enter the next.

For Horses, Horseflies

We know nothing of the lives of others.
Under the surface, what strange desires,
what rages, weaknesses, fears.

Sometimes it breaks into the daily paper
and we shake our heads in wonder –
'Who would behave in such a way?' we ask.

Unspoken the thought, 'Let me not be tested.'
Unspoken the thought, 'Let me not be known.'

Under the surface, something that whispers,
'Anything can be done.'

For horses, horseflies. For humans, shame.

Optimism

More and more I have come to admire resilience.
Not the simple resistance of a pillow, whose foam
returns over and over to the same shape, but the sinuous
tenacity of a tree: finding the light newly blocked on one side,
it turns in another. A blind intelligence, true.
But out of such persistence arose turtles, rivers,
mitochondria, figs – all this resinous, unretractable earth.

Tree

It is foolish
to let a young redwood
grow next to a house.

Even in this
one lifetime,
you will have to choose.

That great calm being,
this clutter of soup pots and books –

Already the first branch-tips brush at the window.
Softly, calmly, immensity taps at your life.

Flowering Vetch

Each of the tragedies can be read
as the tale of a single ripening self,
every character part of one soul.
The comedies can be included in this as well.
Often the flaw is a flaw of self-knowledge;
sometimes greed. For this reason
the comic glint of a school of herring leads to no plot line,
we cannot imagine a tragedy of donkeys or bees.
Before the ordinary realities, ordinary failures:
hunger, coldness, anger, longing, heat.
Yet one day, a thought as small as a vetch flower opens.
After, no longer minding the minor and almost wordless role,
playing the messenger given the letter
everyone knows will arrive too late or ruined by water.
To have stopped by the fig and eaten was not an error, then,
but the reason for going.

Theology

If the flies did not hurry themselves to the window
they'd still die somewhere.

Other creatures choose the other dimension:
                                                                to slip
into a thicket, swim into the shaded, undercut
part of the stream.

                              My dog would make her tennis ball
disappear into just such a hollow,
pushing it under the water with both paws.
Then dig for it furiously, wildly, until it popped up again.

A game or a theology, I couldn't tell.

The flies might well prefer the dawn-ribboned mouth of a trout,
its crisp and speed,
                              if they could get there,
though they are not in truth that kind of fly
and preference is not given often in these matters.

A border collie's preference is to do anything entirely,
with the whole attention. This Simone Weil called prayer.
And almost always, her prayers were successful –
                                                                      the tennis ball
could be summoned again to the surface.

When a friend's new pound dog, diagnosed distempered,
doctored for weeks, crawled under the porch to die, my friend
          crawled after,
pulled her out, said, 'No!',

as if to live were just a simple matter of training.
The coy-dog, startled, obeyed.
Now trots out to greet my car when I come to visit.

Only a firefly's evening blinking outside the window,
this miraculous story, but everyone hurries to believe it.

Vilnius

For a long time
I keep the guidebooks out on the table.
In the morning, drinking coffee, I see the spines:
St Petersburg, Vilnius, Vienna.
Choices pondered but not finally taken.
Behind them – sometimes behind thick fog – the mountain.
If you lived higher up on the mountain,
I find myself thinking, what you would see is
more of everything else, but not the mountain.

Burlap Sack

A person is full of sorrow
the way a burlap sack is full of stones or sand.
We say, 'Hand me the sack,'
but we get the weight.
Heavier if left out in the rain.
To think that the sand or stones are the self is an error.
To think that grief is the self is an error.
Self carries grief as a pack mule carries the side bags,
being careful between the trees to leave extra room.
The mule is not the load of ropes and nails and axes.
The self is not the miner nor builder nor driver.
What would it be to take the bride
and leave behind the heavy dowry?
To let the thin-ribbed mule browse in tall grasses,
its long ears waggling like the tails of two happy dogs?

In a Room with Five People, Six Griefs

In a room with five people, six griefs.

Some you will hear of, some not.

Let the room hold them, their fears, their anger.

Let there be walls and windows, a ceiling.

A door through which time

changer of everything

can enter.

The Bell Zygmunt

For fertility, a new bride is lifted to touch it with her left hand,
or possibly kiss it.
The sound close in, my friend told me later, is almost silent.

At ten kilometers, even those who have never heard it know what it is.

If you stand near during thunder, she said,
you will hear a reply.

Six weeks and six days from the phone's small ringing,
replying was over.

She who cooked lamb and loved wine and wild-mushroom pastas.
She who when I saw her last was silent as the great Zygmunt mostly is,
a ventilator's clapper between her dry lips.

Because I could, I spoke. She laid her palm on my cheek to answer.
And soon again, to say it was time to leave.

I put my lips near the place a tube went into
the back of one hand.
The kiss – as if it knew what I did not yet – both full and formal.

As one would kiss the ring of a cardinal, or the rim
of that cold iron bell, whose speech can mean 'Great joy',
or – equally – 'The city is burning. Come.'

It Was Like This: You Were Happy

It was like this:
you were happy, then you were sad,
then happy again, then not.

It went on.
You were innocent or you were guilty.
Actions were taken, or not.

At times you spoke, at other times you were silent.
Mostly, it seems you were silent – what could you say?

Now it is almost over.

Like a lover, your life bends down and kisses your life.

It does this not in forgiveness –
between you, there is nothing to forgive –
but with the simple nod of a baker at the moment
he sees the bread is finished with transformation.

Eating, too, is a thing now only for others.

It doesn't matter what they will make of you
or your days: they will be wrong,
they will miss the wrong woman, miss the wrong man,
all the stories they tell will be tales of their own invention.

Your story was this: you were happy, then you were sad,
you slept, you awakened.
Sometimes you ate roasted chestnuts, sometimes persimmons.

GALWAY KINNELL

BOBBBIE BRISTOL

Galway Kinnell's diverse work ranges from odes of kinship with nature to realistic evocations of urban life, from religious quest to political statement, from brief imagistic lyrics to extended, complex meditations. His poetry has always been marked by precise, furious intelligence, by rich aural music, by devotion to the things and creatures of the world, and by transformations of every understanding into singing, universal art. In the citation for the 2003 National Book Award, the judges called Kinnell 'America's preeminent visionary' whose work 'greets each new age with rapture and abundance [and] sets him at the table with his mentors: Rilke, Whitman, Frost'.

In 1982 his *Selected Poems* won a Pulitzer Prize and a National Book Award. An updated and expanded edition was published as *Selected Poems* by Bloodaxe in Britain in 2001. This shows how the traditional Christian sensibility of his early work gives way to the sacramental, transfiguring dimension of the later poetry, which 'burrows fiercely into the self away from traditional sources of religious authority or even conventional notions of personality... Short, chanting lines, a simple, declarative syntax, emphatic rhythms, bleak imagery, and insistent repetition: all are used here to generate the sense of the poet as shaman who throws off the "sticky infusions" of speech and becomes one with the natural world, sharing in the primal experiences of birth and death' (Richard Gray). Like the work of his friends and contemporaries James Wright, W.S. Merwin and Philip Levine, Kinnell's poetry showed an early mastery and then rejection of strict poetic forms, along with a growing tendency to direct the imagination inward, linking a vision of the world to an understanding of the self.

In his essay 'Poetry, Personality, and Death' (1971), Kinnell argued that to avoid the self-absorbed, closed ego of our time, the poet must get beyond personality by going through it, moving 'toward a poetry in which the poet seeks an inner liberation by going so deeply into himself – into the worst of himself as well as the best – that he suddenly finds he is everyone'. Like Wright, he was for a time linked with the American 'deep image' group of poets, whose inspiration included the Spanish *canto jondo* ('deep song'), the work of Lorca and the Symbolist theory of correspondences. But Kinnell took the stylised 'deep image' mode in a new narrative direction. Like the hunter in his celebrated poem 'The Bear', he seeks out the primitive bases of existence obscured by the overlay of modern civilisation. His poems examine the effects of personal confrontation with violence and inevitable death, attempts to hold death at bay, the plight of the urban dispossessed, and the regenerative powers of love and nature. Kinnell is a poet who 'writes about the terror and wonder of human beings: the terror, because we know we must die; the wonder, because we are so capable of love' (Bill Moyers).

Born in Providence, Rhode Island, in 1927, Galway Kinnell grew up on the edge of Pawtucket, as he told Alice Quinn: 'If I went out my front door I would find the Seekonk Lace Mill, but if I went out my back door I would find the forest. I spent a lot of time alone in the forest, and that certainly imprinted what's called the natural world [...] I was probably about 13 or 14 when I discovered that I loved poetry. I would say 99% of the poetry I read I hated. It embarrassed me. That one per cent I loved was Edgar Allan Poe. There was something that I felt in Poe himself that reminded me of me. And the other thing about Poe was that he transformed language – what was in the mouths of us in Pawtucket, where the accent is hardly poetic – into singing. And that's what enraptured me about poetry specifically, that language could sing. I can still recite by heart all of the poems that I loved.' (*The New Yorker*, 30 October 2006).

After serving in the US Navy in 1945-46, he studied at Princeton University – along with Merwin – and after graduating in 1948 took a masters degree at Rochester. From 1949 to 2005 he made his living mostly from teaching, in France, Iran and Australia as well as at colleges and universities across America, as he later recalled: 'Until I was in my 40s, I taught only as an adjunct teacher, getting paid a pittance. Sometimes I would have three universities or colleges lined up at the same time, and then I would spend one day at one place and drive through the night to another. When I had to give a reading, all my money from reading went to hiring a substitute. Especially when my children came along, it was quite difficult.'

Socio-political issues have remained an important element in his poetry, and Kinnell was closely involved in the radical political movements of the 1960s. His fieldwork for the Congress of Racial Equality (CORE), helping to register Southern black voters, and his participation in Vietnam antiwar demonstrations and readings, deepened and broadened his Whitmanian vision of the United States of America. Stirred by his poetry readings and his calls for social activism, Kinnell's students at Juanita College, Pennsylvania took part in the 'Bloody Sunday' march on voting rights in Selma, Alabama in March 1965, which became a turning-point in the history of the civil rights movement when the marchers were attacked by state troopers. *Life Magazine* showed a galvanising image of the violence: a photograph of a tearful black woman tending the wounds of a white man felled while standing in support of black voter rights. The man was Galway Kinnell, clubbed in the face by a deputy he'd been trying to reason with. Such was the national outcry against both the violence and the injustice that President Lyndon Johnson signed a new Voting Rights Act in August 1965. Kinnell's involvement with the civil rights movement and protests against the Vietnam War fed his book-long poem *The Book of Nightmares* (1971).

He has published several translations, including work by Rilke, Villon and Yvan Goll. His translation of Yves Bonnefoy's *On the Motion and Immobility of Douve* was published in the Bloodaxe Contemporary French Poets series in 1992. He was State Poet of Vermont, and his other honours have included a Fulbright scholarship (when he lived in Paris), and Guggenheim and MacArthur fellowships. For many years he was Erich Maria Remarque Professor of Creative Writing at New York University, only retiring in 2005. He lives in Vermont and New York.

His latest collection, *Strong Is Your Hold* (Bloodaxe Books, 2007), includes his long poem 'When the Towers Fell', a requiem for those who died in the World Trade Center on 9/11 in direct view of his New York apartment. The selection of poems here is taken from *Selected Poems* and *Strong Is Your Hold*.

Extracts from interviews with Galway Kinnell

1. JASON HOLLANDER (2005)

JH: You've written a poem to William Carlos Williams, one of your poetic heroes. How did he inspire you? Who else is at the top of your list?

GK: William Carlos Williams was the first well-known poet I came to know in person. I would visit him from time to time and read him my new poems. I felt that he welcomed me into the community of poets, and he also gave me useful advice. Other poets who influenced me were Frost, Yeats, Smart, Poe, Dickinson, Whitman, Clare, Shelley, Keats, Villon, Rilke, plus many poet-friends.

JH: You once said that you believe Emily Dickinson, more fully than most poets, told how it is to be a human being in a particular moment. How did she do that?

GK: Emily Dickinson apparently suffered from bipolar disorder and knew suffering and – through her extraordinary empathy – even death more fully than any poet except possibly Shakespeare. With her extraordinary intelligence, bravery, and recklessness, she went very far. She herself drew a 'haggard comfort' from reading certain poems of others and knowing that there lived some other soul 'by heavenly love forgot'. Her poems sometimes provide this 'haggard comfort' to us.

JH: Do you believe that real suffering, of the kind that Dickinson endured, is an experience necessary for poetry? Are poets who have lived rather happy lives worth reading?

GK: Probably the most useful thing is to have experienced a wide range of emotions, so that one can speak of this or that situation with some authority. As for a happy life, even the happiest lives include loss, a measure of suffering, and the knowledge of death. Aristotle suggests that those who believe they live happy lives should wait until it is all over before declaring it happy.

JH: Has there ever been a time when poetry, as an art form, felt confining to you?

GK: I did once feel that rhyme and meter were confining, but then I discovered Walt Whitman, who set me free. Of all literary forms, poetry is the one I feel is most suited to my way of knowing.

JH: So in what way does poetry give you satisfaction?

GK: Poetry is the one art that asks a person to tell, in words, in the first person, what it is for her or him to live here and now.

2. DANIELA GIOSEFFI (2001)

DG: I want to ask you about this idea of being a "nature poet". Your definition of nature poetry includes urban poetry and the anthills of civilisation.

GK: Yes, but I don't think of myself as a "nature poet". I don't recognise the distinction between nature poetry and – what would be the other thing? – human civilisation poetry? We are creatures of the earth. All the creatures have their intricate ways of living on earth. Humans are unique in one respect: we've taken over. We've taken over so successfully that we've become a threat to many of the other creatures and even a danger to the earth itself, so that's why I don't think of myself as a "nature poet". Poems about other creatures may have political and social implications for us.

DG: Indeed, yours do. And this idea you have often expressed – for example, in an essay on Walt Whitman – that poets can write themselves toward a better self if they are honest in their self-knowledge. Can you say something about that?

GK: If we divide humankind into the good and the bad and put ourselves among the good and others among the bad, we can never write truthful poetry. It's all false if it's based on a false premise. No doubt some people are morally better or worse than some others are, but it is necessary to see that this is not an absolute classification. Knowing that what we call evil in others also exists in ourselves at least makes it possible to write something that has some authenticity.

3. KEN McCULLOUGH (1976)

KMcG: Ralph Mills said: 'Like Roethke or Gary Snyder, Galway Kinnell is attracted to the non-human world…as the basic context of man's living.' Do you agree with this statement?

GK: Well, yes, I do. The nonhuman *is* the 'basic context' of human existence. Some let it come into their poetry more than others. When in the presence of wind, or the night sky, or the sea, or less spectacular instances of the nonhuman – including its revelation through the human – we are reminded both of the kinship and the separation between ourselves and what is beyond us. If there is one kind of moment from which poetry springs. I would say it's this one. Do you know Anne Sexton's poem on the night sky? ['The Starry Night'] It expresses a death wish and yet I think it is strangely life-giving – it expresses what you might call the *happy* hunger to die.

4. WAYNE DODD & STANLEY PLUMLY (1972)

WD/SP: You mentioned briefly Rilke's influence. How about Yeats? How does he come into your poetry?

GK: In my early 20s I thought Yeats was not only the greatest of all poets, but also in a manner of speaking, poetry itself. In everything I wrote I tried to reproduce his voice. If my poems didn't sound like Yeats, I thought they weren't poetry. Of course I was the only one to hear the resemblance. Yeats became a more useful mentor when I began to see his limitations. I think my interest in the poem made of sections, of elements that don't come together until the end, probably derives from Yeats, from poems like 'Among Schoolchildren'. I've always loved how all the materials of that poem come back woven together and transformed. In this way Yeats's more complicated poems resemble the Platonic dialogue.

WD/SP: What is it you find in Rilke, besides his ability to structure the long poem as he does it, that's so apparently influential and dynamic in your own life and work?

GK: Rilke writes only what is a matter of life and death. There's nothing trivial, no bright chatter, no clever commentary. He writes at the limit of his powers. There are moments when he seems to write beyond the limit. His poetry gropes out into the inexpressible, like the late music of Beethoven. [...]

WD/SP: Who do you think you are most like in your handling of free verse, if anyone? You are without question a person very much in the old free verse tradition.

GK: Well, as for influences, I don't know of any poetry whose music has moved me as much as that of Walt Whitman; also the King James Bible.

WD/SP: Did you and Merwin write poems when you were at Princeton and show them to each other?

GK: Yes, we showed each other poems – though mine, by comparison, were crude. Even at 19 Merwin was writing poems of extraordinary skill. His sense of the richness of English, his ear for its music, were then, and remain now even in his leaner poems, superior to anyone's. He was the one who introduced me to Yeats's poetry – he arrived late one night, book in hand, and read Yeats to me until dawn.

Interviews: Jason Hollander, *NYU Today*, May 30, 2005, 18 no.13; Daniela Gioseffi, *Cortland Review*, 17 (August 2001); Ken McCullough (8 February 1976), *Anyart Journal*, 2 no.6 (March 1977); Wayne Dodd & Stanley Plumly (15 May 1972), *Ohio Review*, 14 no.1 (Fall 1972).

The Bear

1

In late winter
I sometimes glimpse bits of steam
coming up from
some fault in the old snow
and bend close and see it is lung-colored
and put down my nose
and know
the chilly, enduring odor of bear.

2

I take a wolf's rib and whittle
it sharp at both ends
and coil it up
and freeze it in blubber and place it out
on the fairway of the bears.

And when it has vanished
I move out on the bear tracks,
roaming in circles
until I come to the first, tentative, dark
splash on the earth.

And I set out
running, following the splashes
of blood wandering over the world.
At the cut, gashed resting places
I stop and rest,
at the crawl-marks
where he lay out on his belly
to overpass some stretch of bauchy ice
I lie out
dragging myself forward with bear-knives in my fists.

3

On the third day I begin to starve,
at nightfall I bend down as I knew I would
at a turd sopped in blood,
and hesitate, and pick it up,
and thrust it in my mouth, and gnash it down,

and rise
and go on running.

4

On the seventh day,
living by now on bear blood alone,
I can see his upturned carcass far out ahead, a scraggled,
steamy hulk,
the heavy fur riffling in the wind.

I come up to him
and stare at the narrow-spaced, petty eyes,
the dismayed
face laid back on the shoulder, the nostrils
flared, catching
perhaps the first taint of me as he
died.

I hack
a ravine in his thigh, and eat and drink,
and tear him down his whole length
and open him and climb in
and close him up after me, against the wind,
and sleep.

5

And dream
of lumbering flatfooted
over the tundra,
stabbed twice from within,
splattering a trail behind me,
splattering it out no matter which way I lurch,
no matter which parabola of bear-transcendence,
which dance of solitude I attempt,
which gravity-clutched leap,
which trudge, which groan.

6

Until one day I totter and fall –
fall on this
stomach that has tried so hard to keep up,
to digest the blood as it leaked in,
to break up
and digest the bone itself: and now the breeze

blows over me, blows off
the hideous belches of ill-digested bear blood
and rotted stomach
and the ordinary, wretched odor of bear,

blows across
my sore, lolled tongue a song
or screech, until I think I must rise up
and dance. And I lie still.

7

I awaken I think. Marshlights
reappear, geese
come trailing again up the flyway.
In her ravine under old snow the dam-bear
lies, licking
lumps of smeared fur
and drizzly eyes into shapes
with her tongue. And one
hairy-soled trudge stuck out before me,
the next groaned out,
the next,
the next,
the rest of my days I spend
wandering: wondering
what, anyway,
was that sticky infusion, that rank flavor of blood, that poetry, by
which I lived?

After Making Love We Hear Footsteps

For I can snore like a bullhorn
or play loud music
or sit up talking with any reasonably sober Irishman
and Fergus will only sink deeper
into his dreamless sleep, which goes by all in one flash,
but let there be that heavy breathing
or a stifled come-cry anywhere in the house
and he will wrench himself awake
and make for it on the run – as now, we lie together,

after making love, quiet, touching along the length of our bodies,
familiar touch of the long-married,
and he appears – in his baseball pajamas, it happens,
the neck opening so small he has to screw them on –
and flops down between us and hugs us and snuggles himself to sleep,
his face gleaming with satisfaction at being this very child.

In the half darkness we look at each other
and smile
and touch arms across this little, startlingly muscled body –
this one whom habit of memory propels to the ground of his making,
sleeper only the mortal sounds can sing awake,
this blessing love gives again into our arms.

Saint Francis and the Sow

The bud
stands for all things,
even for those things that don't flower,
for everything flowers, from within, of self-blessing;
though sometimes it is necessary
to reteach a thing its loveliness,
to put a hand on its brow
of the flower
and retell it in words and in touch
it is lovely
until it flowers again from within, of self-blessing;
as Saint Francis
put his hand on the creased forehead
of the sow, and told her in words and in touch
blessings of earth on the sow, and the sow
began remembering all down her thick length,
from the earthen snout all the way
through the fodder and slops to the spiritual curl of the tail,
from the hard spininess spiked out from the spine
down through the great broken heart
to the sheer blue milken dreaminess spurting and shuddering
from the fourteen teats into the fourteen mouths sucking and blowing
beneath them:
the long, perfect loveliness of sow.

Daybreak

On the tidal mud, just before sunset,
dozens of starfishes
were creeping. It was
as though the mud were a sky
and enormous, imperfect stars
moved across it as slowly
as the actual stars cross heaven.
All at once they stopped,
and, as if they had simply
increased their receptivity
to gravity, they sank down
into the mud, faded down
into it and lay still, and by the time
pink of sunset broke across them
they were as invisible
as the true stars at daybreak.

Blackberry Eating

I love to go out in late September
among the fat, overripe, icy, black blackberries
to eat blackberries for breakfast,
the stalks very prickly, a penalty
they earn for knowing the black art
of blackberry making; and as I stand among them
lifting the stalks to my mouth, the ripest berries
fall almost unbidden to my tongue,
as words sometimes do, certain peculiar words
like *strengths* or *squinched* or *broughamed*,
many-lettered, one-syllabled lumps,
which I squeeze, squinch open, and splurge well
in the silent, startled, icy, black language
of blackberry eating in late September.

The Road Between Here and There

Here I heard the snorting of hogs trying to re-enter the underearth.
Here I came into the curve too fast, on ice, and touched the brake pedal and sailed into the pasture.
Here I stopped the car and snoozed while two small children crawled all over me.
Here I reread *Moby Dick*, skipping big chunks, skimming others, in a single day, while Maud and Fergus fished.
Here I abandoned the car because of a clonk in the motor and hitch-hiked (which in those days in Vermont meant walking the whole way with a limp) all the way to a garage, where I passed the afternoon with ex-loggers who had stopped by to oil the joints of their artificial limbs and talk.
Here a barn burned down to the snow. 'Friction,' one of the ex-loggers said. 'Friction?' 'Yup, the mortgage, rubbin' against the insurance policy.'
Here I went eighty but was in no danger of arrest, for I was blessed – speeding, trying to get home to see my children before they slept.
Here I bought speckled brown eggs with bits of straw shitted to them.
Here I brought home in the back seat two piglets who rummaged inside the burlap sack like pregnancy itself.
Here I heard again on the car radio Handel's concerto transcribed for harp and lute, which Inés played to me the first time, making me want to drive after it and hear it forever.
Here I sat on a boulder by the winter-steaming river and put my head in my hands and considered time – which is next to nothing, merely what vanishes, and yet can make one's elbows nearly pierce one's thighs.
Here I forgot how to sing in the old way and listened to frogs at dusk.
Here the local fortune teller took my hand and said, 'What is still possible is inspired work, faithfulness to a few, and a last love, which, being last, will be like looking up and seeing the parachute opening up in a shower of gold.'
Here is the chimney standing up by itself and falling down, which tells you you approach the end of the road between here and there.
Here I arrive there.
Here I must turn around and go back and on the way back look carefully to left and to right.
For when the spaces along the road between here and there are all used up, that's it.

Prayer

Whatever happens. Whatever
what is is is what
I want. Only that. But that.

That Silent Evening

I will go back to that silent evening
when we lay together and talked in silent voices,
while outside slow lumps of soft snow
fell, hushing as they got near the ground,
with a fire in the room, in which centuries
of tree went up in continuous ghost-giving-up,
without a crackle, into morning light.
Not until what hastens went slower did we sleep.
When we got home we turned and looked back
at our tracks twining out of the woods,
where the branches we brushed against let fall
puffs of sparkling snow, quickly, in silence,
like stolen kisses, and where the *scritch scritch scritch*
among the trees, which is the sound that dies
inside the sparks from the wedge when the sledge
hits it off center telling everything inside
it is fire, jumped to a black branch, puffed up
but without arms and so to our eyes lonesome,
and yet also – how can we know this? – *happy!*
in shape of chickadee. Lying still in snow,
not iron-willed, like railroad tracks, willing
not to meet until heaven, but here and there
treading slubby kissing stops, our tracks
wobble across the snow their long scratch.
So many things that happen here are really little more,
if even that, than a scratch, too. Words, in our mouths,
are almost ready, already, to bandage the one
whom the *scritch scritch scritch*, meaning *if how when*
we might lose each other, scratches scratches scratches
from this moment to that. Then I will go back
to that silent evening, when the past just managed

to overlap the future, if only by a trace,
and the light doubles and casts
through the dark a sparkling that heavens the earth.

Oatmeal

I eat oatmeal for breakfast.
I make it on the hot plate and put skimmed milk on it.
I eat it alone.
I am aware it is not good to eat oatmeal alone.
Its consistency is such that it is better for your mental health if
somebody eats it with you.
That is why I often think up an imaginary companion to have
breakfast with.
Possibly it is even worse to eat oatmeal with an imaginary companion.
Nevertheless, yesterday morning, I ate my oatmeal with John Keats.
Keats said I was right to invite him: due to its glutinous texture,
gluey lumpishness, hint of slime, and unusual willingness to
disintegrate, oatmeal must never be eaten alone.
He said it is perfectly OK, however, to eat it with an imaginary
companion,
and he himself had enjoyed memorable porridges with Edmund
Spenser and John Milton.
He also told me about writing the 'Ode to a Nightingale'.
He wrote it quickly, he said, on scraps of paper, which he then stuck
in his pocket,
but when he got home he couldn't figure out the order of the stanzas,
and he and a friend spread the papers on a table, and they
made some sense of them, but he isn't sure to this day if
they got it right.
He still wonders about the occasional sense of drift between stanzas,
and the way here and there a line will go into the configuration of a
Moslem at prayer, then raise itself up and peer about, then
lay itself down slightly off the mark, causing the poem to
move forward with God's reckless wobble.
He said someone told him that later in life Wordsworth heard about
the scraps of paper on the table, and tried shuffling some
stanzas of his own, but only made matters worse.
When breakfast was over, John recited 'To Autumn'.
He recited it slowly, with much feeling, and he articulated the words
lovingly, and his odd accent sounded sweet.

He didn't offer the story of writing 'To Autumn', I doubt if there is much of one.
But he did say the sight of a just-harvested oat field got him started on it
and two of the lines, 'For Summer has o'er-brimmed their clammy cells' and 'Thou watchest the last oozings hours by hours', came to him while eating oatmeal alone.
I can see him – drawing a spoon through the stuff, gazing into the glimmering furrows, muttering – and it occurs to me:
maybe there is no sublime, only the shining of the amnion's tatters.
For supper tonight I am going to have a baked potato left over from lunch.
I'm aware that a leftover baked potato can be damp, slippery, and simultaneously gummy and crumbly,
and therefore I'm going to invite Patrick Kavanagh to join me.

Last Gods

She sits naked on a boulder
a few yards out in the water.
He stands on the shore,
also naked, picking blueberries.
She calls. He turns. She opens
her legs showing him her great beauty
and smiles, a bow of lips
seeming to tie together
the ends of the earth.
Splashing her image
to pieces, he wades out
and stands before her, sunk
to the anklebones in leaf-mush
and bottom-slime – the intimacy
of the visible world. He puts
a berry in its shirt
of mist into her mouth.
She swallows it. He puts in another.
She swallows it. Over the lake
two swallows whim, juke, jink,
and when one snatches
an insect they both whirl up

and exult. He is swollen
not with ichor but with blood.
She takes him and talks him
more swollen. He kneels, opens
the dark, vertical smile
linking heaven with the underearth
and murmurs her smoothest flesh
more smooth. On top of the boulder
they join. Somewhere
a frog moans, a crow screams.
The hair of their bodies
startles up. At last they call out
in the tongue of the last gods,
who refused to go,
chose death, and shuddered
in joy and shattered in pieces,
bequeathing their cries
into the human throat. Now in the lake
two faces float, looking up
at a great maternal pine whose branches
open out in all directions
explaining everything.

from When One Has Lived a Long Time Alone

1

When one has lived a long time alone,
one refrains from swatting the fly
and lets him go, and one is slow to strike
the mosquito, though more than willing to slap
the flesh under her, and one hoists the toad
from the pit too deep to hop out of
and carries him to the grass, without minding
the poisoned urine he slicks his body with,
and one envelops, in a towel, the swift
who fell down the chimney and knocks herself
against window glass, and releases her outside
and watches her fly free, a life line flung at reality,
when one has lived a long time alone.

7

When one has lived a long time alone,
one likes alike the pig, who brooks no deferment
of gratification, and the porcupine, or thorned pig,
who enters the cellar but not the house itself
because of eating down the cellar stairs on the way up,
and one likes the worm, who by bunching herself together
and expanding works her way through the ground,
no less than the butterfly, who totters full of worry
among the day lilies as they darken,
and more and more one finds one likes
any other species better than one's own,
which has gone amok, making one self-estranged,
when one has lived a long time alone.

9

When one has lived a long time alone,
and the hermit thrush calls and there is an answer,
and the bullfrog head half out of water utters
the cantillations he sang in his first spring,
and the snake lowers himself over the threshold
and slides away among the stones, one sees
they all live to mate with their kind, and one knows,
after a long time of solitude, after the many steps taken
away from one's kind, toward these other kingdoms,
the hard prayer inside one's own singing
is to come back, if one can, to one's own,
a world almost lost, in the exile that deepens,
when one has lived a long time alone.

10

When one has lived a long time alone,
one wants to live again among men and women,
to return to that place where one's ties with the human
broke, where the disquiet of death and now also
of history glimmers its firelight on faces,
where the gaze of the new baby meets the gaze
of the great granny, and where lovers speak,
on lips blowsy from kissing, that language
the same in each mouth, and like birds at daybreak
blether the song that is both earth's and heaven's,
until the sun rises, and they stand
in the daylight of being made one: kingdom come,
when one has lived a long time alone.

Parkinson's Disease

While spoon-feeding him with one hand
she holds his hand with her other hand,
or rather lets it rest on top of his,
which is permanently clenched shut.
When he turns his head away, she reaches
around and puts in the spoonful blind.
He will not accept the next morsel
until he has completely chewed this one.
His bright squint tells her he finds
the shrimp she has just put in delicious.
She strokes his head very slowly, as if
to cheer up each hair sticking up
from its root in his stricken brain.
Standing behind him, she presses
her cheek to his, kisses his jowl,
and his eyes seem to stop seeing
and do nothing but emit light.
Could heaven be a time, after we are dead,
of remembering the knowledge
flesh had from flesh? The flesh
of his face is hard, perhaps
from years spent facing down others
until they fell back, and harder
from years of being himself faced down
and falling back, and harder still
from all the while frowning
and beaming and worrying and shouting
and probably letting go in rages.
His face softens into a kind
of quizzical wince, as if one
of the other animals were working at
getting the knack of the human smile.
When picking up a cookie he uses
both thumbtips to grip it
and push it against an index finger
to secure it so that he can lift it.
She takes him to the bathroom,
and when they come out, she is facing him,
walking backwards in front of him
holding his hands, pulling him

when he stops, reminding him to step
when he forgets and starts to pitch forward.
She is leading her old father into the future
as far as they can go, and she is walking
him back into her childhood, where she stood
in bare feet on the toes of his shoes
and they foxtrotted on this same rug.
I watch them closely: she could be teaching him
the last steps that one day she may teach me.
At this moment, he glints and shines,
as if it will be only a small dislocation
for him to pass from this paradise into the next.

Rapture

I can feel she has got out of bed.
That means it is seven A.M.
I have been lying with eyes shut,
thinking, or possibly dreaming,
of how she might look if, at breakfast,
I spoke about the hidden place in her
which, to me, is like a soprano's tremolo,
and right then, over toast and bramble jelly,
if such things are possible, she came.
I imagine she would show it while trying to conceal it.
I imagine her hair would fall about her face
and she would become apparently downcast,
as she does at a concert when she is moved.
The hypnopompic play passes, and I open my eyes
and there she is, next to the bed,
bending to a low drawer, picking over
various small smooth black, white,
and pink items of underwear. She bends
so low her back runs parallel to the earth,
but there is no sway in it, there is little burden, the day has hardly begun.
The two mounds of muscles for walking, leaping, lovemaking,
lift toward the east – what can I say?
Simile is useless; there is nothing like them on earth.
Her breasts fall full; the nipples
are deep pink in the glare shining up through the iron bars

of the gate under the earth where those who could not love
press, wanting to be born again.
I reach out and take her wrist
and she falls back into bed and at once starts unbuttoning my pajamas.
Later, when I open my eyes, there she is again,
rummaging in the same low drawer.
The clock shows eight. Hmmm.
With huge, silent effort of great,
mounded muscles the earth has been turning.
She takes a piece of silken cloth
from the drawer and stands up. Under the falls
of hair her face has become quiet and downcast,
as if she will be, all day among strangers,
looking down inside herself at our rapture.

Everyone Was in Love

One day, when they were little, Maud and Fergus
appeared in the doorway naked and mirthful,
with a dozen long garter snakes draped over
each of them like brand-new clothes.
Snake tails dangled down their backs,
and snake foreparts in various lengths
fell over their fronts. With heads raised and swaying,
alert as cobras, the snakes writhed their dry skins
upon each other, as snakes like doing
in lovemaking, with the added novelty
of caressing soft, smooth, moist human skin.
Maud and Fergus were deliciously pleased with themselves.
The snakes seemed to be tickled, too.
We were enchanted. Everyone was in love.
Then Maud drew down off Fergus's shoulder,
as off a tie rack, a peculiarly
lumpy snake and told me to look inside.
Inside the double-hinged jaw, a frog's green
webbed hind feet were being drawn,
like a diver's, very slowly as if into deepest waters.
Perhaps thinking I might be considering rescue,
Maud said, 'Don't. Frog is already elsewhere.'

How Could She Not

In memory of Jane Kenyon, 1947–1995

The air glitters. Overfull clouds
slide across the sky. A short shower,
its parallel diagonals visible
against the firs, douses and then
refreshes the crocuses. We knew
it might happen one day this week.
Out the open door, east of us, stand
the mountains of New Hampshire.
There, too, the sun is bright,
and heaped cumuli make their shadowy
ways along the horizon. When we learn
that she died this morning, we wish
we could think: how could it not
have been today? In another room,
Kiri Te Kanawa is singing
Mozart's *Laudate Dominum*
from far in the past, her voice
barely there over the swishings of scythes,
and rattlings of horse-pulled
mowing machines dragging
their cutter bar's little reciprocating
triangles through the timothy.

This morning did she wake
in the dark, almost used up
by her year of pain? By first light
did she glimpse the world
as she had loved it, and see
that if she died now, she would
be leaving him in a day like paradise?
Near sunrise did her hold loosen a little?

Having these last days spoken
her whole heart to him, who spoke
his whole heart to her, might she not
have felt that in the silence to come
he would not feel any word
was missing? When her room filled
with daylight, how could she not

have slipped under a spell, with him
next to her, his arms around her, as they
had been, it may then have seemed,
all her life? How could she not
press her cheek to his cheek,
which presses itself to hers
from now on? How could she not
rise and go, with sunlight at the window,
and the drone, fading, deepening, hard to say,
of a single-engine plane in the distance,
coming for her, that no one else hears?

Insomniac

I open my eyes to see how the night
is progressing. The clock glows green,
the light of the last-quarter moon
shines up off the snow into our bedroom.
Her portion of our oceanic duvet
lies completely flat. The words
of the shepherd in *Tristan*, 'Waste
and empty, the sea,' come back to me.
Where can she be? Then in the furrow
where the duvet overlaps her pillow,
a small hank of brown hair
shows itself, her marker that she's here,
asleep, somewhere down in the dark
underneath. Now she rotates
herself a quarter turn, from strewn
all unfolded on her back to bunched
in a Z on her side, with her back to me.
I squirm nearer, careful not to break
into the immensity of her sleep,
and lie there absorbing the astounding
quantity of heat a slender body
ovens up around itself.
Her slow, purring, sometimes snorish,
perfectly intelligible sleeping sounds
abruptly stop. A leg darts back

and hooks my ankle with its foot
and draws me closer. Immediately
her sleeping sounds resume, telling me:
'Come, press against me, yes, like that,
put your right elbow on my hipbone, perfect,
and your right hand at my breasts, yes, that's it,
now your left arm, which has become extra,
stow it somewhere out of the way, good.
Entangled with each other so, unsleeping one,
together we will outsleep the night.'

Why Regret?

Didn't you like the way the ants help
the peony globes open by eating the glue off?
Weren't you cheered to see the ironworkers
sitting on an I-beam dangling from a cable,
in a row, like starlings, eating lunch, maybe
baloney on white with fluorescent mustard?
Wasn't it a revelation to waggle
from the estuary all the way up the river,
the kill, the pirle, the run, the rent, the beck,
the sike barely trickling, to the shock of a spring?
Didn't you almost shiver, hearing book lice
clicking their sexual dissonance inside an old
Webster's New International, perhaps having just
eaten out of it *izle*, *xyster*, and *thalassacon*?
What did you imagine lies in wait anyway
at the end of a world whose sub-substance
is glaim, gleet, birdlime, slime, mucus, muck?
Forget about becoming emaciated. Think of the wren
and how little flesh is needed to make a song.
Didn't it seem somehow familiar when the nymph
split open and the mayfly struggled free
and flew and perched and then its own back
broke open and the imago, the true adult,
somersaulted out and took flight, seeking
the swarm, mouth-parts vestigial,
alimentary canal come to a stop,

a day or hour left to find the desired one?
Or when Casanova took up the platter
of linguine in squid's ink and slid the stuff
out the window, telling his startled companion,
'The perfected lover does not eat.'
As a child, didn't you find it calming to imagine
pinworms as some kind of tiny batons
giving cadence to the squeezes and releases
around the downward march of debris?
Didn't you glimpse in the monarchs
what seemed your own inner blazonry
flapping and gliding, in desire, in the middle air?
Weren't you reassured to think these flimsy
hinged beings, and then their offspring,
and then their offspring's offspring, could
navigate, working in shifts, all the way to Mexico,
to the exact plot, perhaps the very tree,
by tracing the flair of the bodies of ancestors
who fell in this same migration a year ago?
Doesn't it outdo the pleasures of the brilliant concert
to wake in the night and find ourselves
holding each other in our sleep?

W.S. MERWIN

DON J. USNER

W.S. Merwin may be the most influential American poet of the last half-century – an artist who has transfigured and reinvigorated the vision of poetry for our time. While he has long been viewed in the States as an essential voice in modern American literature, his poetry was unavailable in Britain for over 35 years until Bloodaxe's publication of his *Selected Poems* in 2007. This new selection covers over five decades of his poetry, from *A Mask for Janus* (1952) to *Present Company* (2005), plus new work. Most of the book is drawn from his major American retrospective, *Migration*, winner of the 2005 National Book Award for Poetry.

His poetry has moved beyond the traditional verse of his early years to revolutionary open forms that engage a vast array of influences and possibilities. As Adrienne Rich wrote of Merwin's work: 'I would be shamelessly jealous of this poetry, if I didn't take so much from it into my own life.'

Merwin has been awarded most of the principal prizes in American poetry, including the Pulitzer Prize, the Bollingen Prize and the Tanning Prize, and a Lannan Lifetime Achievement Award.

As well as being an internationally renowned poet, he is the author of many classic translations, including editions of Neruda, Follain, Dante's *Purgatorio*, *The Song of Roland, The Poem of the Cid*, and (from Bloodaxe) *Sir Gawain and the Green Knight.* His translations also fed his own experiments with metre and form, with influences ranging from the symbolism of W.B. Yeats and Wallace Stevens to the surrealism of Neruda, Jean Follain's linguistic innovation and Robert Graves's writings on myth. Ezra Pound (whom he met at 19) told him 'to regard writing not as a matter of inspiration (in the occasional sense) but rather as a spontaneity which arises out of discipline and continual devotion to something...What I've chosen to translate is as much a matter of affinities I recognised as I went along as of influences on what I wrote' (Bourne interview, 1982).

Born in 1927 in New York City, the son of a Presbyterian minister, William Merwin began writing hymns at the age of five. He grew up during the Depression in Union City, New Jersey, and in Scranton, Pennsylvania. At Princeton, on a scholarship, he was taught by John Berryman and R.P. Blackmur, and later spent a postgraduate year studying Romance languages. He recalls his early youth in a recent memoir, *Summer Doorways* (2005), much of which covers his time in Europe just after the war.

After working as a tutor in France and Portugal, Merwin moved to Mallorca in 1950 (where he tutored a son of Robert Graves), and then to London in 1951, making a living for a some years in Britain as a translator and BBC scriptwriter. In 1952, his first collection, *A Mask for Janus*, won the Yale Younger Poets prize, selected by W.H. Auden, who praised the young poet's technical virtuosity. As playwright-in-residence at the Poet's Theatre, Cambridge, Massachusetts, in 1956-57, he got to know Robert Lowell, Sylvia Plath, Ted Hughes, Adrienne Rich and Donald Hall.

The 1960s saw him experimenting with metrical irregularity and indirect narration, as described in his essay 'On Open Form' (1969). This attempt to write 'more directly' was not appreciated by some critics who called his work 'hopelessly obscure', as he later explained: 'They thought it was wilfully obscure and that I was trying to write incomprehensible poetry. I was really trying to make it more direct but at the same time more inclusive, to make it contain more experience and to transmit it more directly in words and do it in a way that carried more of the cadences of speech.'

His recent poetry is perhaps his most personal, arising from his deeply held beliefs. Merwin is not only profoundly anti-imperialist, anti-war and environmentalist, but also possessed by an intimate feeling for landscape and language and the ways in which land and language interflow. His latest poems are densely imagistic evocations of life in time and of the natural world. Bill Moyers has described how Merwin 'distances himself from the assumption that human beings are superior to other living things. Animals have taught him important lessons about moral virtues and ways of being...A growing concern for human beings' separation from and destruction of nature has shaped his poems and environmental activism.'

His many books include *The Ends of the Earth* (2004), a gathering of essays expressing the breadth of his fascination with the natural world and the explorers who have journeyed through it. He now lives in Hawaii on the island of Maui, where he tends to his writing and to his garden of rare and endangered palm trees.

from A Conversation with W.S. Merwin
by DANIEL BOURNE

DB: The Seventies seemed a time of political relaxation, or at least part of it did. Was it for you? Do you think your poetry seemed to turn away a bit...?

WSM: It depends on what you mean by politics. If you mean concern with the manipulation of human beings by other human beings, if you want to define it that way, you could say that's true. I was trying to say last night that what organised human activity is doing to the world is the same thing it's doing to language and culture around us and to other cultures, to other people and species. The natural world is inseparable from us, and our attitude toward it, our use of it, is political action. If you pick up any part of it you pick up the whole thing. Sometimes I feel more immediately concerned with what's happening to the elements, the sea, the animals, the language, than I do with any particular society. I don't make a distinction in terms of importance. The poisoning of the soil, the imminence of nuclear disaster, are the same thing. You shut your eyes and you open them and you're staring at the same thing though the form of it may look different.

DB: Do you think you are influenced or have any sort of affinity for Robinson Jeffers? [...] In many ways, both of you seem to be dealing with the same perspective, but you're attacking it in completely different ways.

WSM: I feel close to his feelings about our human self-importance, which I think is one of the things strangling us, our own bloated species-ego. The assumption that human beings are different in kind and in importance from other species is something I've had difficulty accepting for 25 years or so. I think our importance is not separable from the rest of life. If we say we are the only kind of life that's of any importance, we automatically destroy our own importance. Our real importance is our capacity for responsibility for every form of life, the recognition that we are a part of the entire universe. We're not the only valuable thing that's ever appeared in the universe.

from Interview with W.S. Merwin
by BEN GEORGE

BG: Many readers are probably aware that your father was a Presbyterian minister. What influence do you think the biblical rhythms of language you grew up with had on your poetry?

WSM: I can't be sure what influence they had, but I know that I loved listening to the King James Version of the Bible. I'm not a Christian and I'm not a subscriber to the Abrahamic covenant tradition, although I was brought up in it and I read a lot of Christian literature, obviously. There are really things of such beauty in the King James Bible. I used to know long passages by heart.

BG: I wonder whether your poetry ever caused any friction in your family, whether your father's Christianity was something against which you had to battle as a young poet. [...]

WSM: By the time I got to college, I was pretty far away from it. But my father was away as a chaplain in the army by then. I studied Christianity some years later, and as I read things like Eckhart and the Mystics, the kind of Christianity that most appealed to me, in a way, was Greek Orthodoxy, mainly because of the contemplative tradition there. Its rigidity and the role of women in it put me off. [...] One of the things that distresses me in our time is that, somewhere along the line (and I see it in Western religions), we've separated ourselves – or tried to persuade ourselves that we're separated – from the rest of life, which I think is sad and dangerous.

BG: I wonder if the problem comes from the idea in the Abrahamic tradition of Adam having dominion over the animals rather than a communion with them.

WSM: I think it does. It's not this way in every mythology. I think the clue in that story is in the expulsion from the garden, which represents separation from the rest of life.

BG: I sense a journey in your poetry with respect to your attitude toward the environment. *The Lice*, as many have noted, is incredibly angry. Later on, in *The Rain in the Trees*, there's a kind of irony, where the speaker, after addressing the devastation of the earth and of trees, says 'but what do I know I am only a witness'. And in *The Pupil*, there's almost a kind of acceptance. In the poem 'In Time' the speaker remembers dancing and feeding oysters to his companion on 'the night the world was about to end'. It's a celebration in the midst of apocalypse – completely antithetical in spirit, it seems to me, to *The Lice*. It reminds me of the quote from Thoreau you mentioned elsewhere, where after the Concord Common was closed he said, 'I didn't pay enough attention to it while it was free.' I get the sense that this is the attitude you want to have toward the natural world now. Is this right?

WSM: Both things are still there. There's the ceaseless effort to save what can be saved. The pessimism of *The Lice* is a presence to me now every bit as dark as it was then, but I see two sides to it. When we destroy the forests, we are destroying ourselves, and this is something that we don't see. I think we are destroying ourselves. There was a recent book about what happened at Easter Island. It's a real agar plate of what we're doing everywhere around the planet. I don't feel optimistic about that at all. On the other hand, if we get stuck in our despair about the whole thing, if that's all we see, then we've allowed the destruction to take us over completely. It's very important to see that in every moment there's the other thing, too, which is that each of us is a part of the world as a whole. Whatever happens to the world as a whole, the great privilege is to have this moment in the continuity of existence. [...] We can't separate ourselves from the fate of the world, but at the same time, I want to remain aware of what's unique and precious about it...

W.S. Merwin: in his own words

Poetry is impossible. You are trying to make your language do something it never did before... It's never done quite satisfactorily. It's a most extraordinary exercise.

*

Absolute despair has no art, and I imagine the writing of a poem, in whatever mode, still betrays the existence of hope, which is why poetry is more and more chary of the conscious mind, in our age.

*

I don't have any ideological sense of what is Merwinlike or un-Merwinlike. I'm always happy to find I'm writing a poem which is different from anything I've written before, but I don't think you can really write out a paradigm. To be surprised is to find new directions and new regions you haven't been into yet, to be surprised by your own writing, that's what I would always be hoping for.

*

Everything's got to do with listening. Poetry is physical. As Pound said, poetry has one pole in reason and one pole in music. It's like making a joke. If you get one word wrong at the end of a joke, you've lost the whole thing.

*

I had a great difficulty putting the actual, ephemeral, phenomenal fact into a poem – because I was interested in the universality of it. It's the way the fact is heard or seen that counts.

*

I write on things that demand on my grief, pain, wonder, and awe.

*

Where injustice prevails (and where does it not?) a poet endowed with the form of conscience I am speaking about has no choice but to name the wrong as truthfully as he can, and to try to indicate the claims of justice in terms of the victims he lives among. The better he does these things the more he may have to pay for doing them.

*

Put at its simplest, and with its possible implications laid out all plain and neat, the decision to speak as clearly and truthfully and fully as possible for the other human beings a poet finds himself among is a challenge to obscurantism, silence, and extinction. And the author of such a decision, I imagine, accepts the inevitability of failure as he accepts the inevitability of death. He finds a sufficient triumph in the decision itself, in its deliberate defiance, in the effort which it makes possible, the risks it impels him to run, and in any clarity which it helps him to create out of the murk and chaos of experience.

Interview with W.S. Merwin by Ben George: recorded in Vancouver, 1 April 2005 in Vancouver: from *Fugue* no. 29 (summer 2005); see extract at http://www.uidaho.edu/fugue/WSMerwin.htm. *A Conversation with W.S. Merwin* by Daniel Bourne (transcribed by Don Boes) from *Artful Dodge*, 3 no. 3 (Fall 1982): see http://www.wooster.edu/artfuldodge/interviews/merwin.htm. *Merwin: In his own words*: gathered by Copper Canyon Press from a profile in *The New York Times*, the Daniel Bourne interview in *Artful Dodge*, several Merwin essays and a colloquium at Stanford on Merwin's poetry.

Learning a Dead Language

There is nothing for you to say. You must
Learn first to listen. Because it is dead
It will not come to you of itself, nor would you
Of yourself master it. You must therefore
Learn to be still when it is imparted,
And, though you may not yet understand, to remember.

What you remember is saved. To understand
The least thing fully you would have to perceive
The whole grammar in all its accidence
And all its system, in the perfect singleness
Of intention it has because it is dead.
You can learn only a part at a time.

What you are given to remember
Has been saved before you from death's dullness by
Remembering. The unique intention
Of a language whose speech has died is order,
Incomplete only where someone has forgotten.
You will find that that order helps you to remember.

What you come to remember becomes yourself.
Learning will be to cultivate the awareness
Of that governing order, now pure of the passions
It composed; till, seeking it in itself,
You may find at last the passion that composed it,
Hear it both in its speech and in yourself.

What you remember saves you. To remember
Is not to rehearse, but to hear what never
Has fallen silent. So your learning is,
From the dead, order, and what sense of yourself
Is memorable, what passion may be heard
When there is nothing for you to say.

Grandmother Watching at Her Window

There was always the river or the train
Right past the door, and someone might be gone
Come morning. When I was a child I mind
Being held up at a gate to wave
Goodbye, goodbye to I didn't know who,
Gone to the War, and how I cried after.
When I married I did what was right
But I knew even that first night
That he would go. And so shut my soul tight
Behind my mouth, so he could not steal it
When he went. I brought the children up clean
With my needle, taught them that stealing
Is the worst sin; knew if I loved them
They would be taken away, and did my best
But must have loved them anyway
For they slipped through my fingers like stitches.
Because God loves us always, whatever
We do. You can sit all your life in churches
And teach your hands to clutch when you pray
And never weaken, but God loves you so dearly
Just as you are, that nothing you are can stay,
But all the time you keep going away, away.

My Friends

My friends without shields walk on the target

It is late the windows are breaking

My friends without shoes leave
What they love
Grief moves among them as a fire among
Its bells
My friends without clocks turn
On the dial they turn
They part

My friends with names like gloves set out
Bare handed as they have lived
And nobody knows them
It is they that lay the wreaths at the milestones it is their
Cups that are found at the wells
And are then chained up

My friends without feet sit by the wall
Nodding to the lame orchestra
Brotherhood it says
on the decorations
My friend without eyes sits in the rain smiling
With a nest of salt in his hand

My friends without fathers or houses hear
Doors opening in the darkness
Whose halls announce

Behold the smoke has come home

My friends and I have in common
The present a wax bell in a wax belfry
This message telling of
Metals this
Hunger for the sake of hunger this owl in the heart

And these hands one
For asking one for applause

My friends with nothing leave it behind
In a box
My friends without keys go out from the jails it is night
They take the same road they miss
Each other they invent the same banner in the dark
They ask their way only of sentries too proud to breathe

At dawn the stars on their flag will vanish

The water will turn up their footprints and the day will rise
Like a monument to my
Friends the forgotten

The River of Bees

In a dream I returned to the river of bees
Five orange trees by the bridge and
Beside two mills my house
Into whose courtyard a blind man followed
The goats and stood singing
Of what was older

Soon it will be fifteen years

He was old he will have fallen into his eyes

I took my eyes
A long way to the calendars
Room after room asking how shall I live

One of the ends is made of streets
One man processions carry through it
Empty bottles their
Image of hope
It was offered to me by name

Once once and once
In the same city I was born
Asking what shall I say

He will have fallen into his mouth
Men think they are better than grass

I return to his voice rising like a forkful of hay

He was old he is not real nothing is real
Nor the noise of death drawing water

We are the echo of the future

On the door it says what to do to survive
But we were not born to survive
Only to live

For the Anniversary of My Death

Every year without knowing it I have passed the day
When the last fires will wave to me
And the silence will set out
Tireless traveller
Like the beam of a lightless star

Then I will no longer
Find myself in life as in a strange garment
Surprised at the earth
And the love of one woman
And the shamelessness of men
As today writing after three days of rain
Hearing the wren sing and the falling cease
And bowing not knowing to what

For a Coming Extinction

Gray whale
Now that we are sending you to The End
That great god
Tell him
That we who follow you invented forgiveness
And forgive nothing

I write as though you could understand
And I could say it
One must always pretend something
Among the dying
When you have left the seas nodding on their stalks
Empty of you
Tell him that we were made
On another day

The bewilderment will diminish like an echo
Winding along your inner mountains
Unheard by us
And find its way out

Leaving behind it the future
Dead
And ours

When you will not see again
The whale calves trying the light
Consider what you will find in the black garden
And its court
The sea cows the Great Auks the gorillas
The irreplaceable hosts ranged countless
And foreordaining as stars
Our sacrifices

Join your word to theirs
Tell him
That it is we who are important

A Contemporary

What if I came down now out of these
solid dark clouds that build up against the mountain
day after day with no rain in them
and lived as one blade of grass
in a garden in the south when the clouds part in winter
from the beginning I would be older than all the animals
and to the last I would be simpler
frost would design me and dew would disappear on me
sun would shine through me
I would be green with white roots
feel worms touch my feet as a bounty
have no name and no fear
turn naturally to the light
know how to spend the day and night
climbing out of myself
all my life

Birdie

You don't think anything that I know of
but as for me when I think of you
I don't know how many of you there are
and I suppose you thought there was just the one

how many times you may have been born
as my father's other sisters would say
in your bawdy nobody is interested
in things like that in the family

somebody wrote down though that you was
born one time on April 20
1874 so that my grandmother
at that occasion was thirteen and the hardest thing
to believe in that account as I think of it
is that she was ever thirteen years old
the way we grew up to hide things from each other

so she had a little baby at that age

and that was you Birdie that was one of you
did you know
it presents a different picture of my
grandmother from the one I was brought up to

that was the you she had when she was thirteen
which goes a long way to explain her
puritanism and your gypsy earrings
and all the withered children who came after
and their scorn of your bright colors and your loud heart

and maybe even your son who was delicate
and an artist and painted heads of Jesus
on church walls where they crumbled and could not be moved
and your having a good time and dying in Arizona

except that as everybody knew
that you
was nothing but a mistake in
the writing and the real Birdie came along
when Grandma was into her twenties and she
had her firstborn a little baby girl
which explains nothing

puritanism earrings the children who came after
your son the frail artist the crumbling heads of Jesus
the having a good time and dying in Arizona
that was the you I met one morning in summer
whom nobody could explain for you was different

inviting all them so unexpected
and not heard of for so long your own mother
younger brother younger sisters new nephew
to breakfast laughing and waving your hands

with all the rings and them not listening
saying they was in a hurry to drive farther
and see the family and you going on
telling them everything there was to eat

Yesterday

My friend says I was not a good son
you understand
I say yes I understand

he says I did not go
to see my parents very often you know
and I say yes I know

even when I was living in the same city he says
maybe I would go there once
a month or maybe even less
I say oh yes

he says the last time I went to see my father
I say the last time I saw my father

he says the last time I saw my father
he was asking me about my life
how I was making out and he
went into the next room
to get something to give me

oh I say
feeling again the cold
of my father's hand the last time

he says and my father turned
in the doorway and saw me
look at my wristwatch and he
said you know I would like you to stay
and talk with me

oh yes I say

but if you are busy he said
I don't want you to feel that you
have to
just because I'm here

I say nothing

he says my father
said maybe
you have important work you are doing
or maybe you should be seeing
somebody I don't want to keep you

I look out the window
my friend is older than I am
he says and I told my father it was so
and I got up and left him then
you know

though there was nowhere I had to go
and nothing I had to do

Unknown Forebear

Somebody who knew him
ninety years ago
called him by a name
he answered to

come out now they said to him
onto the porch and stand
right there

it was summer and the nine windows
that they could see
were open all the way
so was the front door
and the curtains faded as aprons hung
limp past the sills while he stood
there alone in his dark suit
and white beard in the sunshine

he appeared to know where he was
whose porch that was and whose
house behind him
younger than he was
and who had opened the windows

and who had left the ladder
propped in the branches up the lane
and the names of his children and their children
and the name of the place
with the pine tree out front
and the mullein a foot high growing
on the green bank
beyond the stones of the walk

as he stood still looking out
through the opening in the painted
picket fence
one tall picket one short picket
all the way along

and no gate in the opening

Late Spring

Coming into the high room again after years
after oceans and shadows of hills and the sounds of lies
after losses and feet on stairs

after looking and mistakes and forgetting
turning there thinking to find
no one except those I knew
finally I saw you
sitting in white
already waiting

you of whom I had heard
with my own ears since the beginning
for whom more than once
I had opened the door
believing you were not far

Place

On the last day of the world
I would want to plant a tree

what for
not for the fruit

the tree that bears the fruit
is not the one that was planted

I want the tree that stands
in the earth for the first time

with the sun already
going down

and the water
touching its roots

in the earth full of the dead
and the clouds passing

one by one
over its leaves

Losing a Language

A breath leaves the sentences and does not come back
yet the old still remember something that they could say

but they know now that such things are no longer believed
and the young have fewer words

many of the things the words were about
no longer exist

the noun for standing in mist by a haunted tree
the verb for I

the children will not repeat
the phrases their parents speak

somebody has persuaded them
that it is better to say everything differently

so that they can be admired somewhere
farther and farther away

where nothing that is here is known
we have little to say to each other

we are wrong and dark
in the eyes of the new owners

the radio is incomprehensible
the day is glass

when there is a voice at the door it is foreign
everywhere instead of a name there is a lie

nobody has seen it happening
nobody remembers

this is what the words were made
to prophesy

here are the extinct feathers
here is the rain we saw

Waves in August

There is a war in the distance
with the distance growing smaller
the field glasses lying at hand
are for keeping it far away

I thought I was getting better
about that returning childish
wish to be living somewhere else
that I knew was impossible
and now I find myself wishing
to be here to be alive here
it is impossible enough
to still be the wish of a child

in youth I hid a boat under
the bushes beside the water
knowing I would want it later
and come back and would find it there
someone else took it and left me
instead the sound of the water
with its whisper of vertigo

terror reassurance an old
old sadness it would seem we knew
enough always about parting
but we have to go on learning
as long as there is anything

In Time

The night the world was going to end
when we heard those explosions not far away
and the loudspeakers telling us
about the vast fires on the backwater
consuming undisclosed remnants
and warning us over and over
to stay indoors and make no signals

you stood at the open window
the light of one candle back in the room
we put on high boots to be ready
for wherever we might have to go
and we got out the oysters and sat
at the small table feeding them
to each other first with the fork
then from our mouths to each other
until there were none and we stood up
and started to dance without music
slowly we danced around and around
in circles and after a while we hummed
when the world was about to end
all those years all those nights ago

To the Soul

Is anyone there
if so
are you real
either way are you
one or several
if the latter
are you all at once
or do you
take turns not answering

is your answer
the question itself
surviving the asking
without end
whose question is it
how does it begin
where does it come from
how did it ever
find out about you
over the sound
of itself
with nothing but its own
ignorance to go by

To the Dust of the Road

And in the morning you are up again
with the way leading through you for a while
longer if the wind is motionless when
the cars reach where the asphalt ends a mile
or so below the main road and the wave
you rise into is different every time
and you are one with it until you have
made your way up to the top of your climb
and brightened in that moment of that day
and then you turn as when you rose before
in fire or wind from the ends of the earth
to pause here and you seem to drift away
on into nothing to lie down once more
until another breath brings you to birth

To the Words

When it happens you are not there

O you beyond numbers
beyond recollection
passed on from breath to breath
given again
from day to day from age
to age
charged with knowledge
knowing nothing

indifferent elders
indispensable and sleepless

keepers of our names
before ever we came
to be called by them

you that were
formed to begin with
you that were cried out
you that were spoken
to begin with
to say what could not be said

ancient precious
and helpless ones

say it

(September 17, 2001)

By Dark

When it is time I follow the black dog
into the darkness that is the mind of day

I can see nothing there but the black dog
the dog I know going ahead of me

not looking back oh it is the black dog
I trust now in my turn after the years

when I had all the trust of the black dog
through an age of brightness and through shadow

on into the blindness of the black dog
where the rooms of the dark were already known

and had no fear in them for the black dog
leading me carefully up the blind stairs